I0418800

PRESSING PAUSE

FINDING REST IN A RESTLESS WORLD

Michael and Selah Hirsch

Pressing Pause: Finding Rest in a Restless World

Copyright © 2025 by Michael and Selah Hirsch

Pressing Pause © is a registered trademark of Sabbath Movement™.

All rights reserved. No portion of this book may be reproduced, stored in a retrieval system, or transmitted in any form or by any means—electronic, mechanical, photocopy, recording, scanning, or other—except for brief quotations in critical reviews or articles, without the prior written permission of the publisher.

Published in Oklahoma City, OK

First Edition: June 2025

ISBN:

Library of Congress Control Number:

Original Artwork by Christa Baca

Photography by Chris Baker and Gracie Allyn

Book Design by Oakes Creative House

Graphic Design by Noura Maloloy-on

Scripture quotations marked NIV are taken from THE HOLY BIBLE, NEW INTERNATIONAL VERSION®, NIV® Copyright © 1973, 1978, 1984, 2011 by Biblica, Inc.® Used by permission. All rights reserved worldwide.

Scripture quotations marked NLT are taken from the Holy Bible, New Living Translation, copyright © 1996, 2004, 2015 by Tyndale House Foundation. Used by permission of Tyndale House Publishers, Inc., Carol Stream, Illinois 60188. All rights reserved.

Scripture quotations marked MSG are taken from THE MESSAGE, copyright © 1993, 2002, 2018 by Eugene H. Peterson. Used by permission of NavPress. All rights reserved. Represented by Tyndale House Publishers, Inc.

Scripture quotations marked "Brenton's Septuagint Translation" are taken from The Septuagint Version of the Old Testament: English Translation by Sir Lancelot C. L. Brenton, originally published in 1844. Public domain.

For information about additional resources and special discounts for bulk purchases, visit: www.startsabbath.com.

To all who find themselves craving peace in this chaotic world, *Jesus invites you to pull up a seat at His table.*

Table of Contents

Praise for Pressing Pause

Michael and Selah are carrying a true gift and a movement message about the power of Sabbath.

It is a message that has transformed their family and a rhythm that once embraced can transform yours as well. If you are running and weary I cannot encourage you enough to take a moment to *Pressing Pause* and receive the gift of rest, alignment, and identity.

- *Rabbi Curt Landry, Curt Landry Ministries*

Having led hundreds on trips to Israel, I've seen firsthand how ancient practices come alive in modern hearts.

In *Pressing Pause*, Michael and Selah share the wisdom of Sabbath in practical steps for today's leaders and families. This book will help so many transform their dinner table into an altar of divine encounter.

- *Bishop Robert Stearns, Eagles' Wings*

This book hits a nerve in the best way.

Pressing Pause names a soul deep exhaustion so many of us are facing in high performing and purpose driven lives. It is not an obligation, it is an invitation to reclaim rest as resistance, essential and a much needed lifeline.

- *Dave Coyle*

Pressing Pause is fulfilling a positive end time Isaiah prophecy where the nations will celebrate the ultimate messianic Sabbath.

Michael and Selah Hirsch are providing the foundational tools for Christians to naturally step into the divine invitation that was extended a long time ago.

- *David Nekrutman, The Isaiah Projects and Biblical Excavations*

Whew! As I read this book, it struck me how badly this "good news" needs to be shared.

Right in the Creator's plan for humanity is the rhythm we are meant to follow as beloved humans, yet we have ignored our time to rest or played at it at best... Sabbath (Shabbat) is set aside for blessing! Our Jewish brothers and sisters have known this all along and their practice proves it. Let's join them and not miss out any longer! I encourage you to read Pressing Pause and begin today to mark time with the Spirit the way Scripture teaches. The seventh day is a blessed day! Jump in and find true rest the way our Maker intended, the way Jesus did while he tabernacled with us - and see what happens. Your good, good Father has lots to share with you, his precious child...and with your family.

- *Rev. Emilie Wierda, The Ingathering*

This book is a must do.

Michael and Selah are architecting a better way of living and have the fruit to prove it. They lead with integrity and serve at the highest levels, and what they've written is nothing short of a lifeline. *Pressing Pause* is a call back to what matters most—a return to sacred rhythms, deep connection, and life as God designed it.

- Pastor Calvin Battle, Destiny Christian Center

This book will be life changing to anyone who reads it.

I have known Michael & Selah for more than 10 years. I know the stories and the reasons behind implementing Sabbath and I've had a front row seat to the transformation in their marriage and in their family by protecting that time. Making Sabbath a priority has changed their family for the better and it will do the same for anyone who reads this.

- Chris Baker, Chris Baker Photography

The style of writing is refreshing!

There are so many points that I took away from *Pressing Pause*. The storytelling and compelling call to action narrative has me waiting for part two.

- Rick Washington, International Word Center

Sabbath rest is what we are all looking for.

Michael and Selah show the why and the how to "unwrap the gift" that is pressing pause.

- *Pastor Joey Armstrong, Life.Church Moore, OK*

In *Pressing Pause*, Michael and Selah take readers on the wonderful journey of discovering the Sabbath - God's gift to His creation.

As two very busy, driven and passionate followers of Jesus, they kindly and curiously unfold the deep impacts of practicing a weekly Sabbath. This resource truly will change your life.

- *Pastor Nic Lesmeister, Gateway Center for Israel and Gateway Church*

Michael and Selah are as authentic in writing as they are in their daily lives.

Their transparency in sharing how they found Sabbath, how they practice it and how they invite their children into it gives you a glimpse into their everyday life. A must read!

- *Lulie DiMauro, Out of the Shadows podcast*

This is a beautiful book to remind us to establish powerful, meaningful traditions with our family that will shape the future for generations to come.

- Pam Winters, LTD Leadership Team Development

Michael and Selah offer a bold and heartfelt invitation to acknowledge the damage to our souls and relationships that our well-intended yet frenzied and chaotic rhythms often cause
—and to discover that there is another way. The vulnerability of their personal journey of discovery invites you to embark on your own life-giving journey of finding the rest, connection, and renewal you crave.

- Jeff Darnauer, Mental Health Therapist

I needed this personally and so does my family.
Every reader will benefit, especially as you vulnerably share your own challenges and how pressing pause and practicing regular Sabbath helped you and your family reset your focus on God.

- Brian Chu, Now Hope

Pressing Pause has inspired me to re-evaluate my Sabbath!

In our loud chaotic world, every one of us would be blessed with divine moments and memories if we would learn to push pause each week!

- *Pastor Kathy Farrington, Destiny Christian Center*

Michael and Selah bare their souls in Pressing Pause.

With honesty and wisdom, they confront the destructive force of burnout and invite us into a God-designed rhythm of peace and purpose. This book will challenge you—and change you.

- *Pastor Justin McAuliff, Church of the Redeemer*

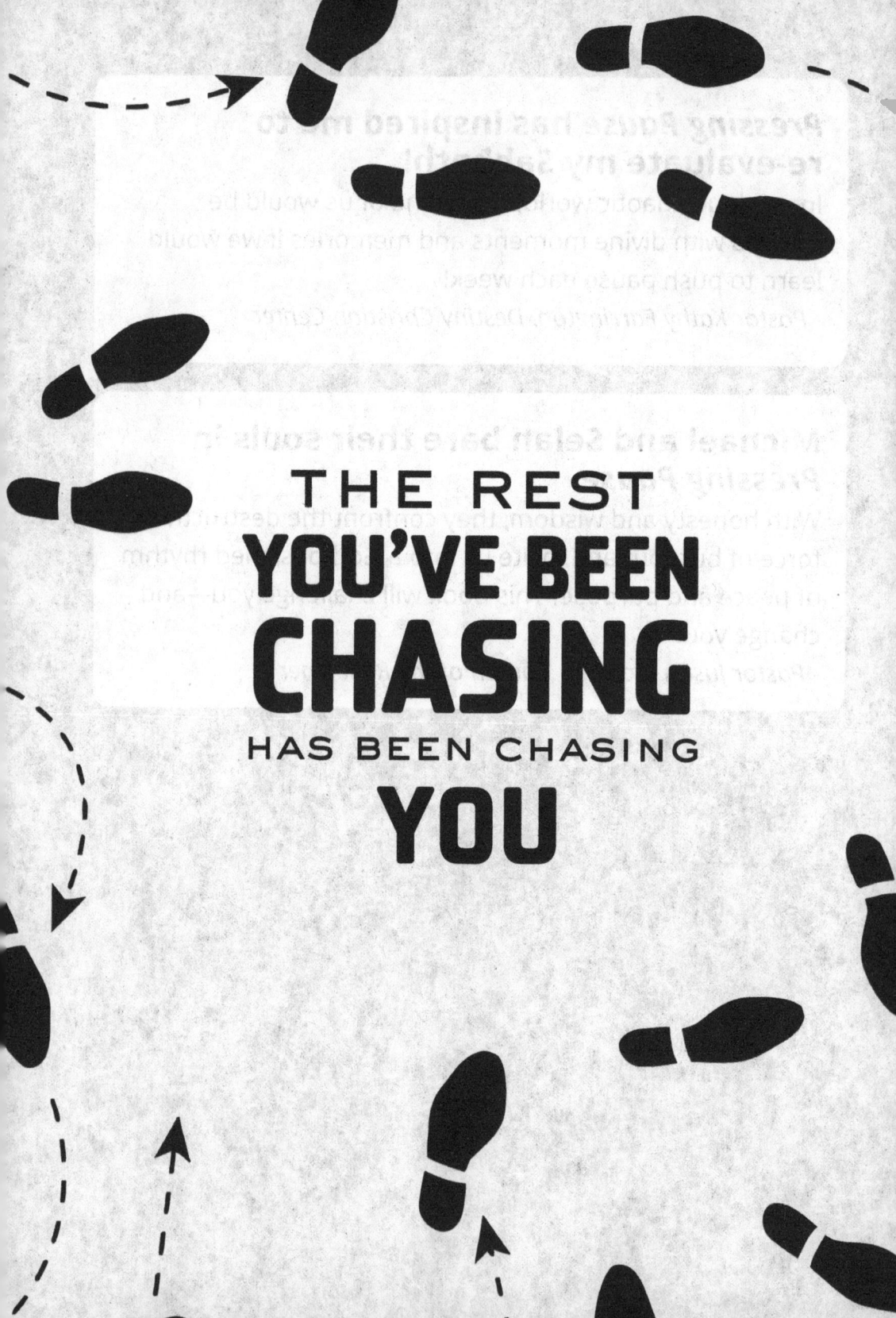

THE REST
YOU'VE BEEN
CHASING
HAS BEEN CHASING
YOU

INTRODUCTION

The Pause Button

You know that moment when your phone battery hits 10%. The red indicator appears, triggering an almost visceral response. Your heart rate quickens. Your eyes dart around for your charger. Which apps can you close? Which messages need a response right now? Suddenly, only the most important things matter.

Our souls have signals too. More subtle, perhaps, but just as real. The difference? We've become masters at ignoring them.

Maybe you recognize these indicators in your own life: the heaviness that settles in your chest on Sunday evenings as another week looms ahead. The short fuse with your children that magnifies all the small things. The creative ideas that once excited you now feel like stale reruns. Prayer that's become a rushed "Help me get through this day, amen."

These warnings alert to sobering realities. The average American checks their phone 144 times daily, surrendering their attention every 10 minutes of waking life.[1] Three-quarters of workers report experiencing burnout.[2]

And perhaps most troubling: despite having faithful spiritual disciplines, nearly 60% of Christians have experienced periods of spiritual doubt.[3]

This isn't just about being tired. It's about losing ourselves in the very life we're working so hard to build.

Week after week, we keep pushing. Meeting deadlines. Managing tasks. Making lunches. Answering emails. Shuttling kids. Maintaining relationships. Scrolling through social media only to see everyone else apparently living with ease and joy. You wonder when exactly life turned into a marathon. You're doing your best but it feels like it's never enough.

What if there's an answer your soul has been desperately searching for? Not another obligation, but the divine connection you were created for.

We understand because we were there too—masters of the hustle, champions of the grind. Two ambitious dreamers and driven leaders who had perfected the art of relentless productivity.

For over a decade, Michael trained for Ironman competitions, waking up at 4 AM to pound out a few hours on the bike trainer and catch a lap swim before the kids were off to school. Gotta give him a shout out for completing 19 races including the world championship! That's 2,671 race miles and about a gazillion training miles! (I, on the other hand, only run to the mailbox!) Then his days would be full of meetings leading nonprofit initiatives that reached tens of thousands of youth across the nation and around the world.

Meanwhile, I've been building a thriving brand agency, working with executives and founders around the world. Immersed in strategy and presentations throughout the day, then switching from CEO to chef to figure out what to cook for dinner. I was literally answering emails while stirring spaghetti. Add to that managing four children's schedules, and our lives were meticulously color-coded from sunrise until we collapsed into bed, exhausted.

But beneath our productive exterior, something was fraying.

Our conversations were becoming increasingly transactional. "Did you pick up the dry cleaning?" "Can you take the kids to practice Thursday?" "Did you respond to that invitation?" Moments with our children felt constantly rushed. "Hurry, get your shoes on." "We're going to be late." "We'll talk about it later."

We were doing all the "right things": church attendance, family dinners squeezed between activities, checking all the boxes of a good Christian life. As followers of Jesus, we thought we had our spiritual rhythm figured out. But beneath the surface? A soul-weariness that no vacation or self-care regimen could touch. An unsettling sense that despite all our activity, we were somehow missing something essential.

The harder we worked to create the life we thought we wanted, the further the peace we truly craved drifted from our grasp.

We were running faster and faster on the wheel of life, but there was this gnawing sense of fulfillment that kept slipping through our fingers. Then, through what we now recognize as divine appointments, we encountered something that transformed our lives from the inside out.

We discovered the gift of Sabbath.

A time to set apart
A time for us to make it all about God
A time to awaken to God's purpose for our lives

Like an airplane ascending on a rainy day, cutting up through dense fog and gray clouds to break above the storm into glimmering sunlight and clear blue skies. Through Sabbath we gain a vantage point impossible to see while caught in the chaos below.

This practice isn't just about stopping work; it's about shifting focus to what truly matters. Not solely focused on refraining from activity, but engaging with eternity. It's both a respite from the world's demands and a remembrance of who we truly are.

We were created for a deep connection with God and with each other. From the beginning, we were designed to find our rest, renewal, and refuge in God. Our souls were made to depend on Him, not to constantly function at full capacity on our own strength. Just as our physical bodies need regular sleep cycles to repair and regenerate, our spiritual lives need renewal through connection with our Creator.

Think about it. When was the last time you experienced a space where the constant pressure to produce and perform was completely suspended? Where your worth wasn't measured by your output? Where you could simply be instead of endlessly doing?

What we discovered wasn't another religious obligation but God's divine pause button—a sacred time where rest leads to delight and propels us toward our purpose.

> "Are you tired? Worn out? Burned out on religion? Come to me. Get away with me and you'll recover your life. I'll show you how to take a real rest" (Matthew 11:28-29 MSG)

When Jesus extended this invitation, He wasn't just speaking of eternal salvation. He was offering a revolutionary approach to living, a way that includes regular rhythms of rest as an act of trust and surrender.

In a world that constantly whispers "more, faster, better," the Father's voice breaks through with a different message, "Come to me. Get away with me." Not as a suggestion, but as a lifeline.

This is an invitation to the very rhythm that will restore your soul to its original design and awaken you to possibilities beyond your imagination. This is the heart of Sabbath.

Let's be honest, stepping off the treadmill of constant productivity, even for a day, can feel terrifying. What will happen to all the plates you're spinning? Who will handle the crises that will inevitably arise? How will everything get done?

These questions haunted us too.

We live in a world charged with chaos. Global conflicts appear daily in news alerts, financial pressures mount with each bill, parenting constantly has its challenges, health concerns lurk in the background. The uncertainty is overwhelming.

What we've discovered is that while we can't control what happens around us, we do have control in how we respond.

Sabbath has become our weekly reset button, not an escape from reality, but a recalibration of our perspective on it. An intentional time to step away from the clamoring to connect with what matters most.

And the most beautiful part? This transformation happens around something as simple and accessible as a table. The same table where you rush through breakfast becomes holy ground. Where you scroll through your phone during lunch becomes a place of sacred connection. Where you eat dinner becomes a sanctuary where souls find nourishment.

When we Sabbath, the ordinary transforms into the sacred.

Phones are put away. The pace slows. Conversation deepens. Eyes meet. Hearts connect. The table, that humble piece of furniture, becomes holy ground where your soul finds nourishment.

After a week of running at full speed, you finally slow down enough to notice, really notice, the people around you. The to-do lists that have been dictating your every move are set aside. The constant pings and notifications fall silent. And in that space, what truly matters comes into crystal-clear focus.

This is an invitation to consider a different way to your usual wake-work-sleep patterns of life.

We're not experts with perfect lives who have it all figured out. We're fellow friends who stumbled upon a hidden treasure and can't help but share its riches. Our Sabbath practice isn't perfect. Many times it's messy. Often it's interrupted. Sometimes it's tearful. But it's always, always worth it.

Little did we know when we first began this journey that we were weeks away from walking into one of the hardest seasons of our marriage. We found ourselves navigating both life and leadership challenges as a series of tests and trials converged into a perfect storm that could have easily capsized our family.

But in those turbulent waters, Sabbath became an anchor. Not because we had perfected an ancient ritual, but because we had created space for God's presence.

Through tears at the table, through weeks when the last thing we felt was peaceful, through moments when we had more concerns and questions than answers, Sabbath held us. It provided the calm within the chaos. It transformed our marriage, parenting, and perspective.

In these pages, we'll share our story of finding renewal amidst the chaos and a depth of connection that has revolutionized the culture of our family. This isn't a quick fix or a 30-day money-back guarantee. **It's a lifestyle of prioritizing your focus and making space for the addition of divine presence.**

Imagine living freer and lighter, not by changing your external circumstances but by changing how you experience them. By keeping company with God, this transforms everything else.

We've crafted this to be read easily and implemented one step at a time. The practice of Sabbath isn't adding another thing to your to-do list. It's about subtracting the unnecessary to discover what matters most. It's about creating space for the essential that gets crowded out by the urgent.

We've broken down this lifestyle into simple steps you can begin immediately, no religious background or special training required. Whether you start with an hour or a full evening, whether your table features takeout or a home-cooked meal, or whether you gather with family or sit in solitude, the promise remains: pressing pause to connect with God will restore what you didn't even realize you'd lost.

Practicing Sabbath will shape:

> The peace in your heart

> The culture of your family

> The legacy you're building

> The way you see the world

> The path you're walking

This isn't about perfect execution. It's about accepting a perfect gift—one meal, one week, one table at a time. We hope you get the courage to start and watch how your Sabbath evolves from awkward first attempts to cherished family traditions.

The invitation before you is to step away from the chaos of constant motion and into the presence of your Creator.

Extraordinary things happen when we dare to pause.

[1] ConsumerAffairs. (2025, March 20). Cell Phone Statistics 2025.

[2] FlexJobs & Mental Health America. (2020, August). Mental Health in the Workplace Survey.

[3] Barna Group. (2023, October 5). Two-Thirds of Christians Face Doubt.

YOUR EXHAUSTION
ISN'T
A
BADGE
OF HONOR
IT'S A
CALL
TO SOMETHING DEEPER

CHAPTER ONE

Warning Lights

Remember when you first got your driver's license? That intoxicating blend of freedom and responsibility. The open road ahead. The promise of adventure. The world suddenly expanded beyond the boundaries of your neighborhood, school, and the places others were willing to drive you.

Back then, the gas gauge was just another dial on the dashboard. Until the signal light flickered on. That orange glow signaled that you're running dangerously close to empty. In those early driving days, running out of gas was just an inconvenience, a rookie mistake, a story to tell later with a laugh.

But now? Now you have people depending on you. Deadlines to meet. Responsibilities that won't wait.

Most of us have experienced that moment of realization: I've pushed it too far this time. Not just in our vehicles, but in our lives. Somehow, we've become experts at ignoring our warning lights, both physical and spiritual.

We know exactly how that feels.

Those who know us well have seen how we like to move through the world. High-octane, full-throttle living was our default setting. Our desire to build organizations, impact thousands, and strive for excellence across multiple ventures became part of our identity.

For nearly 15 years, I've been building my agency—working with CEOs and founders to transform their vision into compelling brands that drive growth. It's work I love, but wow, the pressure of always being 'on' for clients while juggling the behind-the-scenes circus of running a business can be absolutely exhausting.

Beneath that productive exterior, an ache was quietly growing. **I had mistaken constant motion for meaningful purpose.**

We were faithful in all the expected ways: church every weekend, date nights when we could manage them, family meals before evening activities. But something was missing.

The Signs of Spiritual Exhaustion

Spiritual and emotional depletion rarely announces itself with a dramatic crash. Instead, it creeps in gradually, with subtle signs that are easily dismissed or, even more dangerously, celebrated as markers of success.

Beneath the surface, spiritual exhaustion leaves these telling traces:

The fatigue that no amount of sleep cures. "Just need to get through this busy season," we tell ourselves, not recognizing that the "season" has somehow stretched into years. The body keeps sending distress signals while the mind keeps overriding them.

The numbness where emotions feel muted, joy distant. Present in body but increasingly absent in spirit. "I'm just being strong," becomes the rationalization, when in reality, the emotional circuitry is shutting down from overload.

The dryness that turns spiritual intimacy into obligation. "Good morning Lord, bless this day, keep everyone safe, amen." Quick, efficient, shallow faith reduced to a transaction rather than a transformative encounter.

The fog that makes simple decisions overwhelming. Standing in front of the refrigerator, staring blankly at its contents, unable to formulate a dinner plan. Sitting in the driveway, needing several minutes to remember the route home after driving the same path hundreds of times. The brain, designed for creative problem-solving, becomes mired in decision fatigue.

But here's what makes spiritual burnout so dangerous in our culture: these warning signs often masquerade as status symbols. Being exhausted means you're important. Being busy means you're valuable. Being stressed means you're successful. Being unable to be present means you're in demand.

Look around, and you'll see a culture that celebrates the empty tank as a status symbol. "Busy" has become our default response to "How are you?", delivered with that strange mixture of complaint and pride that signals importance. We wear our exhaustion like a badge of honor, evidence that we're needed, valuable, significant.

The very indicators that a soul is in danger have been rebranded as evidence of doing life right.

I remember attending a leadership cohort in a sleek room overlooking the city. Twenty of us sat around a massive mahogany conference table. All high-achievers, all ambitious, all there to share our latest victories and breakthrough strategies.

One by one, we took turns presenting our innovations and impact metrics. The CEO to my left rattled off impressive growth numbers. The nonprofit director across from me described a program that had transformed thousands of lives. The tech entrepreneur next to her casually mentioned a recent funding round that made my head spin.

As each person spoke with polished confidence, I felt myself mentally calculating: Am I doing enough? Am I achieving enough to matter? Have I accomplished something worth mentioning in this room? I found myself sizing up my value the way a kid quickly sizes up the largest cookie on the platter.

I was thinking in a way that God did not intend. Believing that my worth depended on my production.

Many people don't recognize their own spiritual depletion until it's nearly consuming them. The signs are dismissed or explained away until the day when explanations no longer work.

The Hunger Beneath the Hustle

What we didn't realize (what perhaps you haven't realized yet either) was that beneath our frantic pace lay a deeper hunger. We were craving deeper connection: with God, with each other, with what truly mattered. Like Martha in the kitchen, we were 'worried and upset about many things' while missing 'the one thing needed' (Luke 10:41-42 NIV).

We found ourselves sprinting through our days, believing that if we just innovate more, lead better, and optimize every opportunity, we'd finally arrive at the fulfillment that successful leadership promised. We kept pushing our definition of "enough"—enough impact, enough recognition, enough forward momentum to outrun the ache that success couldn't fill.

But the very pace that we thought proved our devotion was actually creating distance from the relationships we valued most.

We were chasing "more" without recognizing that what our souls truly craved was not more activity but divine intimacy.

Our prayer life consisted of hurried requests on the go. "Lord, help me make this deadline." "God, let the traffic clear." "Jesus, don't let me lose my temper in this meeting." Increasingly transactional rather than transformational.

Our marriage conversations toggled between logistics, planning, and problem-solving. "Who's taking the kids to practice?" "Did you pay the mortgage?" "Can you handle the parent-teacher conference?" Necessary information, yes, but hardly the soul-connecting dialogue that romance is built upon.

We sensed there was a depth of relationship, a quality of presence, a richness of spiritual experience that kept eluding us despite our church attendance and consistent devotional practices. But we didn't know how to access it in the midst of our high-velocity life.

Have you felt it too? That creeping emptiness that no promotion, purchase, or accomplishment seems to fill. The strange hollowness that follows checking off every box on your to-do list. The quiet desperation of wondering "is this perpetual exhaustion what life is supposed to feel like?"

You're not alone. And you're not imagining it. Your soul, like your body, was never designed to run indefinitely without reconnecting to its Source.

> "And the peace of God, which transcends all understanding, will guard your hearts and your minds in Christ Jesus"
> (Philippians 4:7 NIV).

We could quote this verse. We've seen it on coffee mugs and bookmarks. But this transcendent peace remained a theological concept rather than a lived experience. Our hearts and minds didn't feel guarded—they felt besieged by constant activity that left little room for divine encounter.

The Achievement Trap

Our culture has trained us to define our worth by our productivity. We've been conditioned to believe that our value is connected to what we can accomplish:

> Good grades earn approval

> Athletic achievements merit celebration

> Career advancement proves our significance

This mentality follows us into adulthood and even shapes our approach to faith. We unconsciously believe that more service, more knowledge, more spiritual disciplines will somehow make us more valuable to God.

But what if our worth to God isn't based on our productivity and everything to do with our identity as His beloved?

In Genesis, humans were declared "very good" not because of anything they had achieved. Their worth was inherent in being made in God's image, not earned through their output.

Yet here we are, God's image-bearers, trying to earn what we already possess: scrambling for approval that was never in question.

This pattern reveals God's heart for our design. We were created for relationship first and foremost. Work is an expression of that relationship, not the basis of it. Our identity as beloved children of God precedes and supersedes any role, responsibility, or achievement.

Are you trying to earn God's approval through your productivity? Trying to be "good enough" for His love through your achievements?

Our souls crave the very connection they were designed to thrive on—the presence of the Father that no amount of achievement can produce. When we step away from constant productivity, even briefly, we declare: "My worth is not in what I produce but in whose I am. My identity is not found in my activity but in being created and loved by God."

Wake Up

Think of it this way: You wouldn't expect your phone to function indefinitely without recharging, right? Yet somehow we've convinced ourselves that we can (that we should) operate continuously without restoration and reconnection to our Creator. **The warning lights in your life aren't nuisances to ignore, they're signals leading you home.** Home to the rest your soul was designed for. Home to the God who never intended for you to run on empty.

> "Dear friend, I pray that you may enjoy good health and that all may go well with you, even as your soul is getting along well" (3 John 1:2 NIV).

This reveals a profound truth: our spiritual and physical wellbeing are meant to be in harmony. In the space created by sacred rest comes the recovery of wonder, the awakening of imagination, the rekindling of creativity. These gifts can only flourish when we create margins for divine encounter.

The first step on our journey isn't just recognizing exhaustion. It's realizing there is more than the need for physical rest; we need soul rest. It's surrendering the striving and waking up to the replenishment that can only come from genuine connection with our Creator.

Do you feel like you are living in permanent low battery mode? This invitation to start Sabbath is simply to receive what's already been given to you.

But here's what we never saw coming: we'd been overlooking the sacred invitation our entire lives.

HOLY

SUBTRACTION

CREATES SPACE FOR THE

ADDITION

OF MEANINGFUL
CONNECTION

CHAPTER TWO

Beautiful Awakening

For us, our awakening didn't come in one dramatic moment. It wasn't a health crisis or relationship ultimatum. It came through what we now call "divine breadcrumbs"—a series of unexpected moments that led us to a journey transforming our relationship with God in ways we never expected.

Like most significant spiritual discoveries, ours began with beautiful mystery: that unique feeling of being bewildered yet drawn in simultaneously. When you don't understand something fully but sense its significance, your heart opens to possibilities you'd never consider if you thought you had all the answers.

Have you ever been to an event where everyone else seems to be in the know? Where to sit, when to eat, what to say? That's how I felt the first time we were invited to a friend's home for a "Sabbath dinner."

We arrived to find their dining room transformed with warm candlelight dancing across cloth napkins in place of the cheap paper ones and the rich aroma of freshly baked bread. The atmosphere felt both festive and reverent, like walking into a celebration where something meaningful was about to happen.

What followed was a beautiful but completely foreign ritual: prayers we couldn't pronounce, traditions we didn't understand, symbolic meanings we couldn't grasp. The hosts moved through each element with a practiced rhythm, while we followed along, trying to mirror their movements and murmur the right responses.

As I fumbled through, smiling and nodding at what I hoped were the appropriate moments, I felt like a tourist who had accidentally wandered into someone's wedding. Beautiful? Absolutely. But it felt like something meant for other people, not for us.

The words were foreign, the practices unfamiliar, yet a childlike curiosity began to build inside me. I watched as their children participated not with eye-rolling reluctance, but with genuine delight. I observed how the tensions of the week seemed to visibly melt from our hosts' shoulders as they shifted into this sacred moment.

What struck me most wasn't the ritual itself, but the palpable sense of God's presence in the room. There was something deeper happening than just a dinner with friends—a holy communion that transcended the unfamiliar elements.

An Unexpected Invitation

The email arrived with a subject line that seemed too good to be true: "Invitation: Israel Tour for Ministry Leaders." Like most people keen to be suspicious of internet fortune, I deleted it, assuming it was spam— the spiritual equivalent of a foreign prince promising millions for my banking details.

A few weeks later, the same invitation appeared again. This time, curiosity won. I opened it and discovered it was real. And extraordinary. Twenty-five pastors were being invited on a fully-funded trip to explore the biblical foundations of our faith, walking where Jesus walked.

There was only one problem: my passport had expired three months earlier.

What followed was a comedy of last-minute madness: expedited renewals, frantic phone calls, and daily check-ins at the mailbox wondering, "Is it here yet?" Each day hoping for a manila envelope that would make the impossible possible. I finally held the fresh passport in my hands just 48 hours before the scheduled departure, still warm from the delivery truck.

As I studied the itinerary on the long flight, I mentally highlighted all the significant stops. The Sea of Galilee where Jesus calmed the storm. The Mount of Beatitudes where He delivered His most famous sermon. The Garden of Gethsemane where He prayed before His crucifixion. Archaeological sites that would bring Scripture to vivid life.

Buried in the middle of the schedule was a simple line item for Friday evening: "Shabbat (Sabbath) Dinner with local family." I barely gave it a passing thought. After all, it wasn't one of the "important" biblical sites on my must-see list.

It wasn't until our guide shared about the significance of Sabbath during one of our daily briefings that I felt a first stirring of interest. **I had never really considered before that Sabbath made God's top ten list—right there between not taking His name in vain and honoring your parents.** He described it not as a religious ritual but as a sacred rhythm that has sustained Jewish families and Christians through centuries of both peace and persecution.

That Friday afternoon, we visited the Western Wall just before sunset. I was struck by the fervency of people praying, their earnest devotion was palpable as they prepared for Sabbath to start. There was an electricity in the air, a sense of holy anticipation I couldn't quite explain but could certainly feel.

Later that evening, our group gathered in a home where a local Orthodox Jewish family welcomed us with extraordinary hospitality. What struck me immediately was the generosity of this invitation: here was a family who had faithfully preserved this sacred tradition for generations, now opening their doors to a group of Christian ministers, eager to share the treasure they had guarded so carefully.

As the sun began to set, our hosts lit two candles on the table and a transformation occurred before my eyes. The ordinary dining room became a sacred space. The family's demeanor shifted from casual to reverent. Time seemed to slow down as they moved through ancient prayers and blessings with the practiced grace of those who had embraced this rhythm countless times before.

I watched, transfixed, as the father placed his hands on his wife's shoulders and each child's head, speaking words of blessing that had echoed through centuries. I observed the intentional pauses between elements, allowing each moment to hold honor for the tradition. I witnessed how the pressures and urgencies of the week melted away as they entered this sacred time together. My heart gained a new revelation that this was the rhythm their ancestors had protected through exile, persecution, and unimaginable hardship.

This wasn't a performance for tourists. This was authentic communion with God and each other, practiced weekly for generations. Now graciously shared with strangers who had found their way to this table. The prayers were in Hebrew, but the peace in that room needed no translation. Their faithfulness to this ancient rhythm had created the very sanctuary my soul was desperately seeking.

It was because of this family's dedication to honoring Sabbath, their choice to guard this sacred time week after week, year after year, that I was able to witness something that would transform my life forever. Little did I know that around a humble table in Jerusalem, not at the historic landmarks I'd been anticipating, God would speak most clearly to my heart through the faithful witness of His chosen people.

Fast forward a few days, as we started our travel back to the states, I called Selah from the airport in Tel Aviv...

"Selah, you won't believe what happened!" The excitement in Michael's voice was unmistakable. This wasn't the enthusiasm of a tourist sharing stories, but the wonder of someone who'd encountered something that shifted everything.

Through the phone, I could almost see his blue eyes dancing as he described the experience, not as a cultural observation or tourist attraction, but as a true revelation. The intentional pause. The connection around the table. The sacred separation of time.

"I want to bring this home," he enthusiastically declared. "I want our family to experience this!"

Knowing my husband's passion and his love for new spiritual discoveries (and his tendency to dive into the deep end without checking the water temperature first), I laughed and said, "Sounds great, babe. Just keep it simple!"

Spoiler alert: He did not keep it simple.

(If you want to skip ahead, check out Chapter Eight where we break down simple steps to start your own Sabbath practice.)

The Beautiful Disaster

Michael returned from Israel like Moses from the mountain. Not with stone tablets, but with books, resources, and pages of notes in his journal.

Within days, he had sketched out our first Sabbath dinner with the meticulous planning he usually reserved for race training. Hebrew phrases were spelled out on note cards. The symbolic meaning of each element was researched. He even practiced the traditional blessings, determined to get the pronunciation just right.

His excitement wasn't merely about trying something new. It was about creating space for an encounter with God that he'd experienced and wanted to bring to our family.

Our first attempt at Sabbath looked more like an awkward first date than a sacred experience. Michael stumbled over an unfamiliar flow. Our kids stared at us with that look "our parents have officially lost it" that every child perfects by age nine.

Candle wax dripped onto the table. The flow felt mechanical rather than sacred. We fumbled through the blessing over the children, with our son asking mid-prayer, "How much longer is this going to take?" The carefully prepared dinner turned cold. But the bread was delicious (who doesn't love bread!).

It was, by most measures, a beautiful disaster.

But here's what happened: We tried again the next Friday. And the Friday after that. Each time, we simplified. We customized. We let go of doing it "right" and focused on what brought genuine connection to our family.

What motivated our persistence wasn't a sense of religious obligation, but a growing hunger for that sacred space of communion with God and each other that we'd glimpsed, however imperfectly, in our first attempt.

The Moment It Clicked

I'll never forget when I realized Sabbath had transformed from a curious exploration to become part of our family's spiritual DNA.

It was a few months into our journey, during one of those weeks that seemed determined to break us. Work deadlines had suddenly accelerated. The kids were locked in what felt like Olympic-level bickering. The dishwasher needed emptying and stacks of dirty dishes piled high in the sink. Our dogs had discovered one of the children's stuffed animals and shredded its stuffing throughout the house like confetti.

By Friday afternoon, I was beyond exhausted. The thought of preparing a special meal felt as impossible as climbing Everest in flip-flops. I was mentally rehearsing how to gently suggest we skip our Sabbath dinner—just this week. Just this once. We'd pick it back up when life calmed down (whenever that mythical time might arrive).

Before the words could leave my lips, our ten-year-old appeared in the kitchen doorway, eyes bright with anticipation. "Mom, can I help set the table for Sabbath tonight? I want to put out the special cups."

Watching her face, I realized this wasn't obligation but anticipation. She wasn't enduring a family ritual but treasuring it. This was something she genuinely looked forward to, a weekly highlight that had already taken root in her heart.

The moments we most want to skip communion with God are usually the times our souls most desperately need it.

That evening, despite the chaos swirling around us, we gathered at our table. The prayers weren't polished. The hastily assembled meal wouldn't have impressed anyone on social media. But as we lit the candles and their gentle light filled the room, something shifted in the atmosphere of our home. As we spoke blessings over each person, as we broke bread together without hurry or agenda, a peace settled over us.

It was the tangible fulfillment of the promise in Philippians, peace that transcends understanding, guarding hearts and minds in a world intent on assaulting both.

From Spectators to Participants

Over time, it dawned on me that we had crossed an invisible threshold from curious spectators to committed participants. This wasn't someone else's tradition anymore; it had become ours. Shaped by our chaos, sanctified by our consistency, and treasured by our children.

What had begun as a dinner experiment had become the rhythm our family's heart beat to. **This went beyond just something new we'd added to our lives. It was a holy subtraction that created space for the addition of divine presence.**

What we were discovering wasn't a religious ritual tucked away in the Old Testament, but a practice Jesus honored and restored to its original purpose: creating space for communion with the Father. And here's the beauty of it: you don't need to visit Israel or learn Hebrew or master any techniques to experience this same transformation at your table.

Sabbath is the gift God gave us we didn't even know we needed.

The invitation had been waiting since the beginning of time, as close as our own dining table. No complicated requirements. No perfect performance expected. Just a willingness to pause and discover what our soul has been craving all along.

Where's God Leading You?

As you've heard our story, I wonder what breadcrumbs has the Lord been dropping in your own life? What gentle invitations have you noticed but perhaps dismissed? What stirrings in your heart have you felt but haven't yet followed?

Maybe it's a longing for deeper connection with your family. Perhaps it's an ache for more authentic connection and communion with God. It could be a growing awareness that the pace of your life is stealing something precious from your soul.

God is always pursuing our hearts, always calling our attention to areas where He wants to meet us more deeply. The Father is actively working in your life right now by opening doors and creating divine appointments.

The question is: are you paying attention? Are you willing to follow the path, even when it feels somewhere unfamiliar?

For us, following God's invitation led to a gift we never saw coming. One that little did we know would become our steady ground in the storm that was about to hit.

SABBATH ISN'T
ESCAPISM
IT'S

SANCTUARY
IN THE
STORM

CHAPTER THREE

Anchored in the Storm

It's not a matter of if you will experience a storm in life, but more a matter of when (or maybe you're going through one right now).

When our storm hit, we had no warning. That's often how life's challenges arrive. We were happily sailing along with no idea of the gale-force winds gathering just over the horizon.

The storm began with a devastating loss that shattered my confidence in ways I never could have anticipated. Still reeling from that, a few weeks later, a leadership crisis erupted, stripping away not just my position but my identity, calling, and financial security in a single crushing moment. Dreams I'd invested years building suddenly collapsed under the weight of circumstances beyond my control.

What followed was a cascade of mounting pressures: decisions about immediate survival and long-term direction, relationship tensions that tested every bond, sleepless nights filled with endless replaying of conversations and scenarios. The raging cycle of shoulda-coulda-woulda, desperately wishing for a redo that would never come.

Then in the midst of all of that, just weeks later, an unexpected life change triggered a season of depression for Selah. This added another layer of darkness to an already suffocating cloud of uncertainty that had settled over our future.

We were drowning. Gasping for air.

We had no idea that the very practice we'd just begun would become the thing that held us together. For us, Sabbath became our anchor.

We had established a rhythm of regularly showing up in God's presence, regardless of how we felt or what was happening around us. When everything else in our lives seemed to be breaking loose, we had those sacred hours. The world's demands were temporarily suspended, and we could remember who we were beyond our challenges.

This anchor held us through a season that could have destroyed us. It provided stability not by calming the waters, but by connecting us to something stronger than the storm.

The Design of the Anchor

Have you ever watched a small boat riding out a storm? It rises and falls with each wave. The rain pelts its deck. The wind still howls through its rigging. But if it's properly anchored, it doesn't crash against the rocks or get swept out to sea. The anchor keeps the boat where it needs to be until the storm passes.

That's exactly what Sabbath does for us in the storms of life.

I've been thinking a lot about anchors lately. Did you know most anchors work not by their weight but by their design? The flukes, those pointed parts at the end, dig into the seabed, and the more pressure applied from above, the deeper they dig in. The anchor doesn't stop the storm, but actually uses the storm's force to create stability.

The very pressure that threatens to destroy the vessel becomes the force that drives the anchor deeper.

This is the surprising power of Sabbath in challenging seasons. The pressures that could pull us away from God's presence actually drive us into greater dependence on Him. The storms that threaten to sweep us away can instead secure us more firmly to the bedrock of what matters most.

You don't prepare for a crisis when you're in one. The habits you've established in calmer waters are what carry you when the seas get rough. We've found no habit more life-preserving than the weekly rhythm of pressing pause to anchor ourselves in God's presence.

When Waves Crash

What's most disorienting about the storms we faced wasn't just their intensity, but how quickly they stripped away our carefully constructed identities. When you've defined yourself by achievement, influence, and accolades, who are you when those things are suddenly taken away?

But it wasn't just the practical pressure that threatened to sink us. It was the questions that crashed against our faith with each passing day. Had we misheard God's calling? Were we on the wrong path entirely? Were these failures a reflection of our leadership, our character, our worth?

In this moment of crisis, we discovered there were essentially three ways we could respond:

Push harder. Believing that more effort, more hustle, more control will somehow fix what's broken.

Check out. Look for ways to numb the pain through distraction, addiction, or disengagement.

Find an anchor. Grab a hold of something solid when everything is shifting. Not a denial of reality, but a stable place from which to face it.

Friday evenings became our lighthouse. We'd gather at our table, light two small candles, and speak the ancient words that had become our language: "Blessed are You, Lord our God, King of the universe." Simple words that reminded us who was actually in charge—and it wasn't us. That's how Sabbath became our anchor.

I remember one Sabbath evening vividly. The day had been particularly brutal. More difficult conversations. More decisions we were unsure of. More nights of tossing and turning, running scenarios over and over.

We gathered at the table. The kids, sensing the heaviness, were unusually quiet. When it came time for blessings, my voice struggled to find something to be grateful for in the midst of such uncertainty.

Then our daughter Nya, just ten at the time, looked up and said with complete conviction: "I'm thankful that God takes care of us even when we don't know how He's going to do it." In that moment, it was as if a spotlight illuminated what really mattered. The storm hadn't diminished. The waves were still crashing, the wind still howling. But our anchor had dug deeper. We were being held secure not by our circumstances but by something far more substantial.

In the midst of chaos, Sabbath was the sanctuary in the storm.

Sometimes we came with tears.
Sometimes with anger.
Sometimes with numb exhaustion.

But we came.

And in that coming, something happened that's difficult to articulate but impossible to deny: **we were held by something larger than ourselves—by the steady, faithful presence of God who promised to meet us there.**

Was it a denial of reality? Not at all. The bills were still there. The difficult decisions couldn't be avoided. Nothing about our circumstances had changed. But for those sacred hours, we gained a perspective that simply wasn't available in the churning waters of our daily concerns. **From that anchored place, the same problems looked different. Not smaller, but manageable in the hands of a God bigger than our storm.**

During that season, we learned something crucial: Sabbath doesn't change our circumstances; it changes our relationship to them. Like an anchor that keeps a boat from being dashed against the rocks, Sabbath kept us from being broken by fears that, in the larger perspective, were temporary concerns rather than eternal truths.

In the Darkness of Depression

Not all storms are external. Some of the most violent tempests rage inside us, hidden from view but no less destructive.

For nearly a year, I walked with Selah as she went through a deep season of anxiety and depression. There were weeks when simply getting out of bed felt like climbing a mountain. Her mind, once filled with creative ideas and strategic plans, became a landscape of fog and shadow.

Depression is a peculiar kind of storm. It doesn't just change your circumstances; it changes how you experience everything. Colors seem less vibrant. Conversations require enormous effort. The simplest tasks become monumental challenges.

When you're drowning internally, there's a strange impulse to push away the very people who might throw you a rescue rope.

You don't want to burden them. You convince yourself they'd be better off without the weight of your darkness. You don't want to be seen in your weakness.

The thought of creating a "special" Sabbath evening when she could barely microwave leftovers felt impossible. Setting a beautiful table? Speaking words of blessing? Finding gratitude in the darkness? It seemed almost absurd.

But here's where the anchor held her: Sabbath wasn't something she had to create; it was a rhythm already woven into our family life. The space for God's presence would be created whether she could sense it or not.

During those months, she would often come to the Sabbath table with tears already forming. And in those moments, the practice we had established held her when she couldn't hold herself.

The blessings were reminders of hope. The candlelight reminded her that darkness never has the final word.

One Friday, in the depths of that season, she couldn't bring herself to prepare anything special. She sat at the table, empty-handed and empty-hearted. "I'm sorry," she whispered. I took her hands and said words that became a touchstone: "All that matters is being with God who's already here waiting for you."

The comfort and healing presence of God held her through that heavy and weary season of life. What we discovered in this internal storm was that **Sabbath isn't a practice reserved for perfect circumstances or emotional stability. It's a sacred refuge especially necessary in our most broken, confused, and painful seasons.**

Holding on to Hope

The anchor of Sabbath is part of God's design for our flourishing in a fallen world. I think of Peter, stepping out of the boat into the raging sea. As long as his eyes were fixed on Jesus, he walked on water. The moment he focused on the waves, he began to sink. Sabbath helps us fix our eyes on Jesus when the storms of life would have us fixate on the waves.

This is why it holds us steady in turbulent times:

Sabbath connects the temporal to the eternal. In the midst of crises that feel all-consuming, Sabbath widens our perspective beyond the immediate to the eternal. It reminds us that while our challenges are real, they're not ultimate. There's a bigger story unfolding, and our current chapter isn't the conclusion.

Sabbath provides renewal of perspective. Unlike a one-time retreat or momentary spiritual high, Sabbath returns us to truth on a regular basis. Just as we need to eat daily, not once a month, our souls need regular realignment with reality as God sees it.

Sabbath creates space for presence when we're tempted to run. Our natural response to pain is often avoidance or numbing. Sabbath creates a container for facing our reality in the safe presence of God and those who love us. It invites us to bring our full selves (fears, doubts, confusion) to the table and find them held in grace.

Sabbath reminds us who we are when storms threaten our identity. When crises hit, they often attack our sense of self. Financial struggles make us feel like failures. Health challenges reduce us to patients. Relationship conflicts leave us feeling unlovable. Sabbath continually reconnects us with our identity as God's beloved children.

God Meets Us Where We Are

What storms are you facing right now? Is it a relationship that's grown distant? Financial pressure that keeps you awake at night? A health diagnosis that's shaken your world? A big dream that feels overwhelming in its scope? A project or calling that's stretching you beyond your comfort zone? The exhausting demands of caregiving that never seem to end?

Or perhaps it's not one dramatic crisis but the accumulated weight of a thousand small things: the constant demands, the unending responsibilities, the feeling that you're always running behind, always falling short, always trying to keep too many plates spinning at once.

We didn't have a guidebook for navigating these rough seas. The perfect storm of circumstances brought us to our knees, literally. In the darkest moments, we found ourselves on the floor, out of strategies, out of strength, out of answers.

Have you been there? Are you there now? That place where your usual coping mechanisms fail. Where motivational quotes ring empty. Where even well-meaning advice from friends feels hollow.

Let tears be part of your offering. Some weeks, the most honest thing you can bring to the table is your brokenness. Don't hide your pain; include it. Light the candles through your tears. Speak the blessings through trembling voices. God meets us most powerfully not in our strength but in our vulnerability.

Receive when you cannot give. There will be seasons when you have nothing to offer. In those times, Sabbath becomes less about what you bring and more about what you receive. Let the blessings wash over you. Let God's presence hold you when you cannot hold yourself.

The strength of Sabbath is in showing up again and again to be with God who is already there waiting for you.

Here's what we've discovered: God meets us exactly where we are in that moment of our lives. We're continually evolving as we fight battles, celebrate victories, and navigate the normalcy of everyday life, but every week, He pulls up a seat at our table to meet us. That's where eternity collides with our humanity.

Many weeks, Sabbath feels like a celebration, a feast of joy and gratitude. Other weeks, it feels like a shelter where we hide from the storm until the winds subside. Still other weeks, it feels like a hospital, a space for binding wounds and beginning healing.

The invitation to Sabbath isn't just for fair-weather sailing. It's for the roughest seas, the darkest nights, the most violent storms. When everything else is breaking loose, this anchor holds. When the storms of life threaten to sweep us away, Sabbath consistently connects us to the One who holds all power—the One whom even the wind and waves obey.

But here's what surprised us most: choosing this ancient rhythm in our modern world didn't just change us; it put us at odds with everything around us.

Turns out, rest is revolutionary.

IN A WORLD THAT WORSHIPS BUSY BUSY REST IS THE ULTIMATE ACT OF REBELLION

Chapter Four

The Countercultural Pause

Let's be honest about the water we're swimming in: We live in a culture that worships busy. We wear our packed schedules like gold medals, humblebrag about how little sleep we're getting, and juggle projects like circus performers.

You think we'd wake up and realize how toxic this is.

But the world keeps spinning.

We're the most productive, connected, and entertained generation in human history. We have devices that instantly answer any question, connect us to anyone anywhere, and entertain us endlessly. We can work from beaches, order groceries from bed, and attend meetings in our pajama bottoms (business attire on top, of course).

Yet anxiety, depression, and burnout are at epidemic levels. We're trapped in loneliness while tangled in digital connection—more networked than ever, yet more isolated than any generation before us.

We've convinced ourselves that rest happens when everything else gets done. Which, spoiler alert, is never. There's always another email to answer, another project to start, another room to organize, another milestone to reach.

We've never been more efficient and never felt more depleted.

The Productivity Idol

"I'll sleep when I'm dead" isn't just a saying; it's practically a mantra for many of us.

The idol of productivity demands endless sacrifice: our health, our relationships, our joy, our wonder—all offered on the altar of endless accomplishment. It demands devotion, but delivers only temporary satisfaction.

During a particularly intense season leading our nonprofit, with speaking engagements and organizational demands at their peak, I was explaining to a friend why I couldn't possibly take even a few hours off. As I listed all my responsibilities and commitments, he asked simply: "Do you believe you're more necessary to God's work than God Himself is?"

The question stopped me cold. Not because I consciously believed that, but because my actions revealed a deeper truth: I was living as if the Kingdom of God depended on my constant availability rather than His perfect sovereignty.

Sabbath asserts that our worth comes not from continual achievement but from the finished work of Christ. Each time we press pause on productivity, we're making a counter-cultural declaration: "I am more than what I produce. My identity is rooted in God's love."

This transition from viewing ourselves primarily as producers to seeing ourselves as beloved is not easy.

The productivity idol doesn't surrender its throne without a fight. But with each consistent choice to press pause, to step into sacred rest, to prioritize presence over productivity, we loosen its grip on our hearts and reclaim our true identity as children of God.

A Divine Rebellion

What if pressing pause isn't just a desperate attempt to take a break from real life? What if making room for rest is the most countercultural action we can take in a world bent on relentless motion?

To be countercultural means to deliberately stand against the prevailing values and practices of society. In our achievement-obsessed world, intentionally stopping isn't just unusual—it's revolutionary. It's a direct challenge to a system that measures human worth by output.

When we intentionally pause, it becomes an act of faith that declares "I trust God enough to stop." This isn't just stepping back from work; it's stepping away from being held captive to nonstop production.

I remember the first time I declined a Friday evening dinner meeting with a colleague to protect our Sabbath time. The pressure to conform, to always be available, to demonstrate our commitment through constant accessibility was intense. But holding that boundary became one of the most powerful statements of our values.

This is surrender.

Most of us don't live at the pace of creation; we live at the pace of chaos. We've abandoned the divine rhythm established in Genesis for the frenetic cadence of notification pings and deadline pressures. The Creator of the universe established a pattern of work and rest, yet we somehow believe we can function without the latter.

Hurried motion keeps us skimming the surface of life. Only when we stop can we sink into its depths, where the real treasures lie. Redefining the meaning of productivity. Creating space for the cultivation of relationships. Nurturing wonder and the development of wisdom that only comes through unhurried presence with God.

When you choose to press pause, you're making a declaration that echoes through both visible and invisible realms: "My worth isn't measured by my achievements. I am more than what I produce. I am a human being, not a human doing."

We've learned that rest isn't weakness. It's wisdom. It's not escape from responsibility but the foundation for meaningful engagement with it. It's not avoiding productivity but finding its true source in communion with our Creator.

The world will not applaud this choice. It will push back with urgent deadlines, social pressures, and the fear of missing out. But beyond the resistance lies a gift of immeasurable value: the peace that transcends understanding, the joy that isn't dependent on circumstances, the perspective that transforms how you experience every dimension of life.

The Picture We Couldn't See

Our journey with Sabbath reminds me of a winter when we had several snow days in a row. The kids were excited to eat mounds of pancakes and come in from playing in the snow to mugs of hot chocolate piled high with mini marshmallows. To pass the time, we pulled out some puzzles and cleared our dining room table for the challenge. One puzzle featured a collage of all the favorite sugary cereals from the 70s and 80s—bright cartoon characters, colorful boxes, and the nostalgic brands I loved to eat on Saturday mornings.

For days, we meticulously sorted and connected pieces, putting together the familiar mascots and vibrant colors. We were nearly finished when Selah placed one of the final pieces and suddenly gasped.

"Look!" she exclaimed. "There's a giant silver spoon across the whole puzzle!"

We stepped back, stunned. An enormous shiny spoon ran through the entire image! The very thing that connected all the cereal boxes, yet we'd been too focused on individual pieces to see it.

That's what Sabbath was like for us. It had been right there in Scripture all along, on the very first pages of Genesis, woven throughout the Bible, modeled by Jesus himself—yet we had missed it completely. We had been so consumed with the individual pieces of our faith—church attendance, Bible reading, prayer—that we'd overlooked a central element designed to bring it all together.

Sometimes the most transformative gifts are hiding in plain sight, waiting for us to step back far enough to see the bigger picture and recognize the divine thread that weaves everything into a meaningful whole.

When Rest Feels Like Failure

Let's get real for a moment: in our achievement-oriented culture, intentionally stepping away from productivity can feel not just difficult, but wrong. As if we're somehow failing by choosing rest.

Have you ever set out to do something relaxing, only to have it become another source of stress?

Picture this: It's a perfect Saturday morning. You decide to take a leisurely family walk instead of weekend chores. You imagine meaningful conversations and rejuvenating fresh air.

What actually happens? Thirty minutes negotiating with the kids why they can't bring their entire toy collection. No clean socks anywhere.

Bathroom breaks before reaching the driveway. "How much longer?" before you've gone a block. Your spouse remembers three work emails that "can't wait." You're sweating, irritated, wondering why you didn't just stick to the routine.

That's been our experience too. Our good intentions to relieve stress and enjoy nature's beauty crashed into reality as we struggled with the logistics of children, belongings, and competing attention spans. Soon enough, we were carrying abandoned bikes, balls, and water bottles by the third house down the street.

Yet, amid the chaos (and sometimes the tears), we kept going because something told us the struggle was worthwhile.

But here's what happens when you stay the course, when you push past the initial resistance that comes with any meaningful change: this rhythm of rest becomes the divine pause button our notification-saturated, productivity-obsessed culture desperately needs.

The Awkward First Steps

When we first began setting aside time for Sabbath, it felt like learning a new dance, except we have little to no natural rhythm (we dance like we have two left feet). When Michael returned from Israel, I remember how his eyes sparkled with passion as he unpacked his suitcase and shared his experiences, but all I could think was: How exactly is this going to fit into our already overscheduled lives, and what does this have to do with our relationship with Jesus?

Our first attempts were honestly more stress than rest. We'd prepare for Sabbath only to have our kids fidget and repeatedly whisper how much longer till dinner. The special meal I cooked was met with the universal childhood food critique: "Can I have ketchup?"

One night after a particularly chaotic attempt, with the kids finally in bed, we sat on the couch surrounded by the evidence of our "restful" evening—dishes on the table, candle wax on the tablecloth, and barely-touched dinner.

"Is this really worth it?" I asked, surveying the scene.

Michael reached for my hand, his eyes still holding that conviction I couldn't quite understand yet. "Give it time," he said. "Think about learning to ride a bike. Remember the wobbling, the falls, the scraped knees? But eventually, the training wheels come off and suddenly you're flying."

He was right. Whether it's learning to ride a bike, mastering a new skill, or building a meaningful tradition—the beginning is almost always messy. The first attempt at anything worthwhile often leaves us wondering if we've made a mistake.

Most good things start awkwardly. Excellence doesn't emerge fully-formed; it develops through persistence, not perfection. And authentic communion with God isn't achieved through perfect rituals but through faithful presence.

The Rest Revolution

What we're witnessing today is nothing short of a modern movement as families, churches, and individuals embrace this sacred rhythm. We're witnessing a transformation against the frantic cycle of productivity.

Every phone turned off or silenced is an act of courage. Every blessing spoken is a testimony. Every table set with intention is a declaration.

Together they mark the threshold between chaos and communion. A different way of living where you press pause and start Sabbath.

This countercultural pause isn't just stepping back from work; it's stepping into the presence of the One who designed rest as the pathway to your flourishing. The question is: will you have the courage to step out of the current pulling you toward constant motion and step into the still waters of God's presence?

What awaits beyond the resistance will transform not just your schedule, but your soul. But how exactly does this transformation unfold?

RE⚡T

ISN'T THE ABSENCE OF

BURDEN

BUT THE

PRESENCE OF GOD
WITHIN IT

CHAPTER FIVE

Sacred Rhythms

It takes courage to swim against the current.

After a few weeks of consistent commitment (and by consistent, I mean consistently imperfect), something began to shift. We noticed ourselves looking forward to Friday evenings. The kids started asking, "How many sleeps till Sabbath?" The preparation became less frantic, more intuitive.

The resistance didn't disappear completely. There were still weeks when work deadlines loomed, when children melted down, when life felt too overwhelming to add one more thing.

But we kept showing up. Sometimes with beautiful place settings and home-cooked meals. Sometimes with pizza on paper plates. The form mattered less than the intention: to connect with God, to remember what actually matters. And slowly but surely, over time, **a series of beautiful rhythms emerged that transformed not just our Friday evenings but the entire culture of our family.**

The Space Between

Selah

Ever notice this little word tucked into the Psalms? It appears 74 times in the Bible and means to pause and ponder the truth that has just been spoken or sung. Like a sacred comma in the middle of worship, creating space for God's words to settle deep into our hearts.

Fun fact: My name is Selah, which literally means "pause", and I'm finally learning how!

The first time we encounter *Selah* is in Psalm 3, where David is surrounded by enemies, crying out to God in desperation.

Picture it: A king on the run. His own son is hunting him down. Allies turned traitors. Death threats echoing in his ears.

But here's what's fascinating about David's pattern in the midst of chaos: He presents his raw, honest heart to God. "Lord, how many are my foes! How many rise up against me! Many are saying of me, 'God will not deliver him'" (Psalm 3:1-2 NIV).

Selah.

Stop.

Breathe.

Let that truth settle.

In that sacred space, something shifts. David moves from his circumstances to God's character. "But you, Lord, are a shield around me, my glory, the One who lifts my head high. I call out to the Lord, and he answers me from his holy mountain" (Psalm 3:3-4 NIV).

Selah.

Another pause.

Another breath.

Another moment to let God's truth override fear's lies.

Then David moves to a place of confident trust—the kind that only comes after pressing pause long enough to remember who's really in control. "I lie down and sleep; I wake again, because the Lord sustains me... From the Lord comes deliverance. May your blessing be on your people" (Psalm 3:5, 8 NIV)

Selah.

What David discovered in those *Selah* moments was a divine pattern of pause, ponder, and proceed, which is exactly what we're invited into through Sabbath. David would lay out his difficulty, then pause to remember who God is, then watch for God's response. Sometimes one *Selah* was enough. Sometimes he needed multiple pauses in a single psalm, cycling back to truth again and again until it anchored his soul.

These pauses aren't empty spaces; they're sacred moments where faith transforms from concept to conviction. Where we disrupt the chaos and constant activity by intentionally stepping into God's presence.

It takes abnormal behavior to get to the other side of our normal human struggles and striving. That's what these sacred rhythms offer—a countercultural pattern of living that creates space for divine encounter.

Sacred Rhythms in Motion

The promise remains: as we continue to show up, God continues to transform us from the inside out. As Jesus reminds us in Matthew 6:33, "Seek first his kingdom and his righteousness, and all these things will be given to you as well" (NIV).

We have experienced a pattern of rhythms: pressing pause, finding rest, discovering delight, and activating purpose. **These rhythms flow naturally from one to the next, creating a continuous cycle of renewal that deepens with each week.** Each feeds into the next: pressing pause creates space for finding rest, which opens your heart to discover delight, which naturally activates purpose. That renewed sense of calling leads you back to pressing pause again, not from exhaustion but from wisdom.

This is what we call the Sabbath Soul Cycle, a pattern that will not only transform your schedule but your soul.

Think of it like breathing. You don't consciously think about inhaling and exhaling. Your body naturally moves through the rhythm that sustains life. In the same way, these four movements become a spiritual breathing pattern for your soul.

What's remarkable is how this pattern perfectly addresses our modern struggles. We live in a culture where the idea of rhythmic renewal feels almost revolutionary. Yet God designed us to function in cycles: seasons of planting and harvest, times of activity and rest, moments of engagement and reflection.

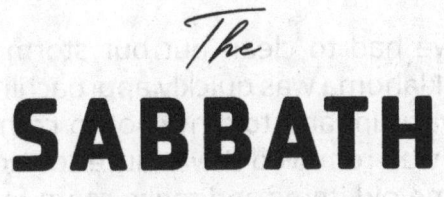

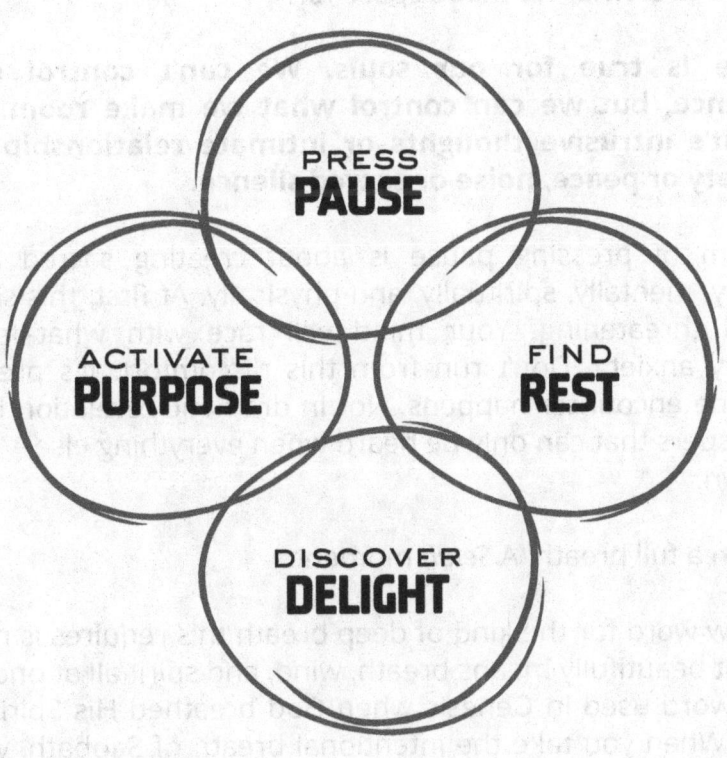

First Rhythm: Press Pause

This rhythm is simple yet revolutionary: make room for God.

A few weeks ago, we had to clean out our storm shelter because tornado season in Oklahoma was quickly approaching. Selah sent me down there with a vacuum and told me not to come out until every creepy crawly thing was removed (I was sure to vacuum twice!). We had to clean out some old items and make room for what was most important in case the storms hit. We couldn't control the weather, but we could control what we made space for.

The same is true for our souls. We can't control every circumstance, but we can control what we make room for— whether it's intrusive thoughts or intimate relationship with God, anxiety or peace, noise or sacred silence.

The rhythm of pressing pause is about creating sacred space emotionally, mentally, spiritually, and physically. At first, this silence might feel threatening. Your mind will race with what-ifs and productivity anxiety. Don't run from this discomfort. It's precisely where divine encounter happens. Not in dramatic revelation but in gentle whispers that can only be heard when everything else quiets down.

You draw in a full breath. A *Selah* moment.

The Hebrew word for the kind of deep breath this requires is ruach. A word that beautifully means breath, wind, and spirit all at once. It's the same word used in Genesis when God breathed His Spirit into humanity. When you take the intentional breath of Sabbath, you're participating in the very act that brought humanity to life.

But here's where trust comes in. Pressing pause requires faith that God is big enough to handle what you can't control while you're creating space for Him.

As Proverbs 3:5-6 reminds us: "Trust in the Lord with all your heart and lean not on your own understanding; in all your ways submit to him, and he will make your paths straight" (NIV).

Sabbath isn't escapism from life's challenges, but from the illusion that we face them alone. Once you've created this threshold of sacred silence, your soul becomes ready to receive the love of the Father.

Second Rhythm: Find Rest

This rhythm is about discovering something profound: finding rest is ultimately about receiving love.

When Jesus came up out of the waters of baptism, before He did anything, before He performed a single miracle or preached a single sermon, the Father's voice broke through the heavens: "This is my Son, whom I love; with him I am well pleased" (Matthew 3:17 NIV). Jesus' identity and belovedness were established before His ministry began.

Later, on the Mount of Transfiguration, God spoke again with the same affirmation: "This is my Son, whom I love; with him I am well pleased. Listen to him!" (Matthew 17:5 NIV). Even perfect, sinless Jesus—needed recurring reminders of His Father's love and pleasure.

If Jesus needed regular affirmation of the Father's love, how much more do we?

Here's the beautiful truth: finding rest isn't about escaping reality or ignoring circumstances. It's about receiving the love that's already been given. It's learning to accept divine shalom as a gift. This Hebrew word means far more than the absence of conflict, it's complete peace and wholeness where your spirit, mind, and body find refuge and restoration in the Father's presence. A good night's sleep refreshes your body, but shalom restores your being.

The world tells us to push harder when we're struggling, to hustle our way through pain, to outwork our problems. But God's economy operates differently. When Jesus saw the crowds "harassed and helpless, like sheep without a shepherd," His response wasn't to give them more to do. It was to invite them to Himself.

There's a beautiful paradox in how rest works. When we've spent ourselves completely, when we have nothing left to give, that's when surrender begins. It's in our emptiness that God's fullness meets us most powerfully.

Rest isn't the absence of burden but the presence of God within it.

The greatest obstacle? Our resistance to receiving when we're conditioned to give, produce, and control. The breakthrough comes when we stop fighting for rest and start surrendering to it, choosing to believe that our worth isn't earned through endless doing but received through simple being. Your mind will spin with everything undone, everyone uncared for, every problem unsolved. For some, finding deep rest takes a few weeks. For others, especially those who have been running on empty for years, it might extend for months.

But finding rest isn't selfish—it's essential. You can't pour from an empty cup. When you receive God's rest, you're positioning yourself to give from abundance, accepting that you are God's beloved.

Third Rhythm: Discover Delight

This rhythm is about experiencing something transformative: joy that emerges from unhurried presence with God.

Six months into our Sabbath practice, life was still challenging. Circumstances hadn't suddenly improved. But as we gathered together that Friday evening, I felt something I hadn't experienced in months: anticipation. Not anxiety about the future, but quiet excitement about the present moment.

One night, our son told a silly story that had everyone laughing until tears streamed down our faces. Our daughter opened up about a dream she'd been afraid to share. We lingered at the table long after the meal was finished, playing a ruthless game of Uno with no regard to time. None of these moments were planned or orchestrated. They emerged naturally from the unhurried space we'd created.

I suddenly realized we were experiencing the fullness of joy. Not because anything had changed externally, but because Sabbath had created a place for our hearts to breathe.

This is discovering delight, the natural fruit that emerges when we stop running long enough to notice beauty, experience genuine joy, and rediscover wonder in God's presence.

Here's where the magic happens. The difference between manufactured happiness and authentic joy is found in conversations that deepen, moments that linger, and laughter that erupts spontaneously. For us, it was the revolutionary act of moving slowly through life while being fully present. When you remove urgency and silence distractions, you create room for genuine presence.

There is something to be found in the margin—the unhurried space that allows connection with God and each other to naturally unfold.

Delight arrives unannounced in ordinary moments marked sacred by intention, a shared meal, gentle candlelight, a child's story told with wild gestures and boundless enthusiasm. The prophet Isaiah calls the Sabbath a delight (Isaiah 58:13). The Hebrew word used here— oneg—means exquisite delight, the kind that makes your soul feel alive. It's central to its purpose.

Here's what you'll discover: when we're caught in the spin cycle of busyness, our vision narrows. We see only our immediate needs, problems, and goals. But in the spaciousness of Sabbath, our perspective expands. We begin to see patterns and possibilities that remain invisible when we're immersed in the minutia.

The Holy Spirit loves to reveal himself when we slow down to honor his presence. Following God's rhythms feels less like following a rigid checklist and more like an adventure, full of unpredictable, surprising, wonder-filled. That's what this rhythm feels like, not a structured religious exercise, but an adventure with God full of joy in the most unexpected places.

This experience of *oneg* is the preparation for releasing your purpose and calling in ways you never imagined possible.

Fourth Rhythm: Activate Purpose

This rhythm is about discovering something powerful: purpose that flows from communion rather than striving.

Ever notice how your best ideas usually never come when you're staring at a screen, frantically paying bills, answering emails, or zipping around running errands? They bubble up naturally in the shower, on walks, while washing dishes—in those quiet, unguarded moments. There's a reason for this: your brain needs space to make connections, see patterns, and synthesize information in unexpected ways.

Sabbath creates that space not just for creativity, but for purpose: for connecting with the deeper why behind all your activity. It's not just about clearing your mind, but about aligning your heart with God's call for your life.

In the unhurried communion with our Creator, we rediscover not just who we are, but why we are. From that place of secure identity, we can engage our work with renewed passion and clarity.

A leader in our network shared something that perfectly captures this rhythm: "What surprised me most was what happened when I finally slowed down. I expected my productivity to drop, but the opposite happened. When I pause, everything changes. The fog lifts. The mental noise quiets down. And the decisions I make from that place? They're wisdom, not reaction. My leadership actually improved when I stopped treating 24/7 availability as a badge of honor."

This is activating purpose, discovering that this fourth rhythm from delight to purposeful action is what sets Sabbath apart from mere relaxation techniques or self-care practices. When we enter into God's presence, we both recover from the week behind us and we become equipped for the work ahead.

Here's what we've experienced: we wake refreshed, renewed, clear. For our family, we found that the days following Sabbath took on a different quality—more focused, more purposeful, more aligned with what really matters. Decisions become easier to make. Priorities order themselves more naturally.

This transformation connects beautifully with Paul's prayer in Ephesians 3:20: "Now to him who is able to do immeasurably more than all we ask or imagine, according to his power that is at work within us" (NIV). When we activate from a place of divine connection rather than personal striving, God's power works through us in ways that exceed our own capacity.

Jesus modeled this in John 17:4, He declares: "I have brought you glory on earth by finishing the work you gave me to do" (NIV). His effectiveness flowed from His connection with the Father, His regular retreats to solitary places for prayer and communion.

This isn't about becoming more productive in the world's eyes but more effective in God's Kingdom. We find ourselves fighting the right battles from the right posture.

This transformation from reactive to proactive, from tactical to strategic, from problem-solver to vision-caster happens through intentional rhythms of engagement and disengagement. It's the inhale that makes the exhale possible. The pulling back of the bow that gives the arrow its flight. The gathering of strength before the leap. The filling of the vessel before it can pour out.

This fourth rhythm completes the Sabbath Soul Cycle, bringing you back to the first with deeper understanding—ready to press pause again, not from exhaustion but from wisdom, knowing this divine rhythm is the foundation for everything meaningful you're called to do.

The Overflow

Here's what we didn't expect when we began this journey: these four sacred rhythms don't stay contained to Friday evening. They overflowed across our lives like water spilling from a fountain that's been filled to overflowing.

Picture a glass being filled under a gentle flowing faucet. At first, the water simply accumulates, bringing the vessel to fullness. But then something beautiful happens—the water reaches the rim and begins to cascade over the edges, pooling onto the surface below, creating ripples that extend far beyond the original container.

That's what happens when these rhythms become integrated into your life. The peace, the perspective, the purpose—they spill over into Monday morning meetings, Tuesday afternoon carpools, Wednesday evening homework battles, and Thursday night dinners.

The peaceful heart you cultivate on Sabbath shows up as patience when your toddler has a meltdown in the grocery store. The generous spirit that emerges from receiving God's love flows into unexpected acts of kindness for neighbors and strangers. The intentional living you practice transforms how you approach ordinary decisions throughout the week.

We've watched this overflow transform our family culture in beautiful ways:

Empathy expands. When you regularly practice blessing each family member, you develop a radar for noticing the goodness in them throughout the week.

Priorities clarify. The perspective gained from stepping back weekly helps you distinguish between urgent and important, between what demands your attention and what deserves it.

Creativity flourishes. The mental and spiritual clarity allows innovative solutions and fresh ideas to emerge in your work and relationships.

Anxiety diminishes. Regular practice of trusting God with your time builds your confidence to trust Him with everyday concerns.

Relationships deepen. The focus of being present with your presence transfers naturally to interactions with colleagues, friends, and extended family.

Each of these four rhythms contributes its own unique overflow:

From **pressing pause** comes the ability to create sacred space in ordinary moments—a brief prayer before a difficult conversation, a conscious breath before responding to stress, a mindful transition between activities.

From **finding rest** comes a peace in your identity that isn't shaken by criticism, setbacks, or unexpected challenges. You carry the Father's love with you into every interaction.

From **discovering delight** comes an awakened capacity for wonder that helps you notice beauty in a sunset, joy in a child's laughter, or gratitude for a perfectly brewed cup of coffee.

From **activating purpose** comes a clarity of mission that transforms your work from mere obligation into meaningful contribution to God's Kingdom.

This overflow is perhaps the most powerful testimony to the transformative nature of Sabbath. People begin to notice something different about you—a peace that doesn't depend on circumstances, a joy that isn't performance-based, a purpose that transcends personal ambition.

The Permission You've Been Waiting For

You have permission to enter these sacred rhythms. Not when everything is finished. Not when you've earned it. Not when life settles down (it won't).

This week. Today. Now.

These rhythms of the Sabbath Soul Cycle create space to feel the Father's touch, to sit in His presence, to tune your ears to His voice.

The enemy of your soul knows that a person connected to their Creator is infinitely more powerful than a person running on their own strength. The resistance you'll feel (and you will feel it) is from a culture that has forgotten the wisdom of rhythms, the necessity of renewal, the intentionality that flows when we press pause.

It all starts with a single *Selah*.

This gift has been waiting since the beginning of creation.

ON THE SEVENTH DAY
WITH THE

CANVAS OF
THE
COSMOS
COMPLETED

GOD
PAUSED

CHAPTER SIX

CHAPTER SIX

Gift of Sabbath

Now that you've heard about the sacred rhythms, you might be wondering: Can something this <u>simple</u> really make that much of a difference?

I get it. The connection with God we'd been chasing had actually been chasing us.

For thousands of years, it had been sitting right there in Genesis, waiting to be unwrapped like the gift it was designed to be. The divine pause button. The sacred rhythm. **The weekly reset our souls were designed for—not just as a break from activity, but as an invitation to intimate communion with our Creator.**

> "And the heavens and the earth were finished, and the whole world of them. And God finished on the sixth day his works which he made, and he ceased on the seventh day from all his works which he made. And God blessed the seventh day and sanctified it, because in it he ceased from all his works which God began to do" (Genesis 2:1-3, Brenton's Septuagint Translation).

I'd read these words countless times without truly seeing them. They weren't just a historical recording of what happened "way back when." They were a divine blueprint for how life is meant to be lived. Before sin entered the world, before the fall, before any commandment was given, God established a tempo of rest and renewal. **It wasn't an afterthought; it was part of the original master design of how we would partner with Him in the ongoing work we are called to.**

What strikes me now is the tenderness behind this rhythm. God's word is not intended to restrict us but to protect us and connect us to His heart. Like a parent who establishes bedtime not to limit a child's fun but to ensure their flourishing, God wove rest into the fabric of creation because He knew exactly what His children needed.

This perspective transformed how we approached Sabbath. It wasn't another spiritual practice to perfect or religious obligation to fulfill. It was a love offering from a Father who understands us better than we understand ourselves.

In the Beginning

> "In the beginning, God created the heavens and the earth. The earth was without form and void, and darkness was over the face of the deep" (Genesis 1:1-2 ESV).

I've read these opening lines of Genesis more times than I can count, but I missed something crucial for years. Before God said "Let there be light," the world was in a state of chaos, formless, empty, dark. The Hebrew words *tohu va-vohu* paint a picture of wild disorder, a cosmic confusion.

God's first creative act wasn't just making stuff appear. It was bringing order from disorder. Peace from chaos. Beauty from emptiness. Form from formlessness. **It was transforming impossibility into infinite possibility revealing what could be where nothing yet existed.**

Does that resonate with where you find yourself right now? Looking at aspects of your life that feel disordered, empty, even dark? Relationships that seem formless? A spiritual life that feels void? A schedule that embodies chaos?

For six days, God sculpted order out of chaos: separating light from darkness, water from land, creating the rhythm of seasons, filling the earth with living creatures. After each day's work, God looked at what He had made and called it "good."

This pattern reveals something we often miss: God created man on day six, which means Adam's first full day of existence was God's day of rest. Before he did anything, before he named a single animal or began tending the garden, he experienced Sabbath with his Creator. **His first assignment wasn't work, it was relationship and communion with God.**

Think about that. The first day of human existence wasn't about productivity—it was about presence. God specifically designed a day to be with the human He had just created. Through that connection would come the activation of Adam's calling. Out of that holy communion, he would then carry out the work God had entrusted to him.

This pattern reveals the divine order: **connection first, then calling. Relationship before responsibility.** Presence before productivity. Our work was always meant to flow from our communion with God, not the other way around.

We are not complete without this regular rest, reset, and renewal in God. We were created to function like a pendulum—the push and pull of work and rest, activity and renewal. Just as a child on a swing needs both the forward motion and the backward retreat to maintain momentum, we need both engagement with our work and disengagement in rest to function as we were designed.

And here's the beautiful revelation we missed: **God gave us rest not as an afterthought but as a vantage point for a deeper relationship with Him.** Perhaps this is why God placed rest at the beginning of human history rather than at the end because without this sacred pause, we can't properly care for and create from the world He's entrusted to us.

The Encore Effect

Have you ever been to a concert or performance that completely transported you? The music swells, the performers give their all, and as the final notes fade, you're on your feet, hands stinging from applause, voice hoarse from cheering. And then, that magical moment when the artists return to the stage for an encore is often the most memorable part of the entire show.

It's called the encore effect. Whether it's the finale of a concert, a firework show, or a speech, you typically save the best for last. It's the thing that you want your audience to remember after the lights go down.

What if God's greatest creative act wasn't making something, but creating an interlude in time so humanity can be in communion with Him? A sacred pause designed for a human being to awaken wonder in God and everything that came before.

Can you imagine being with God near the end of the 6th day? By now, you've seen a magnificent light that we will only get to see in eternity, followed by God creating the sky, dry land, plants and trees, the sun, moon and stars, animals that live on the land, and finally, humans made in His own image.

You would have to be thinking, what could possibly be next? Something big and dramatic is about to happen.

Drumroll please, pull out your smartphones and wave them in the air, and...

God does His own version of the encore effect which is to not just flip the script, but He throws the script away. As the cascading wonders of creation reach their crescendo, God doesn't create something new—He creates space. Not another thing, but time. Not production, but presence.

And here's the kicker: **God doesn't call the seventh day "good" like all the others. He calls it "holy".**

The word *kodesh* in Hebrew, means set apart, transcendent, completely other than ordinary.

It's the first time this word appears in Scripture. Not for the magnificent stars or the majestic mountains or even for humanity. The first thing God declares *kodesh* (holy) is not a thing at all—it's time. Specifically, time set apart for rest and communion with Him. The principle of time management can be found within the very first few pages of the Bible—a divine revelation that how we steward our time matters more than how we organize our tasks.

This is significant when we consider Peter's words centuries later: "But just as he who called you is holy, so be holy in all you do; for it is written: 'Be holy, because I am holy'" (1 Peter 1:15-16 NIV). The same Hebrew concept of *kodesh* that God first applied to Sabbath is what He later calls us to embody in our own lives. When we honor Sabbath, we're not just observing a ritual—we're participating in the very first thing God ever designated as holy, aligning ourselves with His character in a tangible way. Our weekly rhythm of sacred rest becomes an embodied declaration that we too are set apart, called to reflect the God who values presence over endless production.

The language shifts as the 7th day is called "holy".

The posture shifts as on the 7th day God rested.

The time shifts as with the 7th day God completed His work.

At first glance this might not seem like much of an encore. But this divine pattern reveals God's values and priorities. **Here's the revelation: God Himself is the encore! He made day seven to be all about Him.** As much as He wants us to enjoy everything else He created—the majestic mountains, the vast oceans, the intricate beauty of every living thing—He wants us to enjoy Him most. **As children of God, Sabbath is not meant to be "me-time" but "God-time!"**

I remember watching the sunset on the west coast several years ago. The display was breathtaking with brilliant oranges and purples painting the endless ocean as day surrendered to night. But what struck me most wasn't the view itself but the collective hush that fell over the crowd. Hundreds of people, standing in reverent silence, staring into the sky, simply being present to beauty too profound for words.

That moment taught me something about worship. Sometimes the highest praise isn't adding our voice, but silencing it in awe. Not producing more, but being present to what already is.

Sabbath is God's encore to creation. A perfectly wrapped gift after His magnificent performance—not an afterthought, but the culmination. Not merely the absence of work, but the presence of wonder.

This sacred pause wasn't about God needing a break—as Isaiah reminds us, "The LORD is the everlasting God, the Creator of the ends of the earth. He will not grow tired or weary" (Isaiah 40:28 NIV). It was about establishing a pattern for us, His image-bearers, and creating a space where relationship could flourish unhindered by the demands of productivity and responsibility.

God didn't just rest on the seventh day and move on. He wove the rhythm of seven into the very fabric of His relationship with humanity. Every seventh day was to be Sabbath. Every seventh year, the land was to rest. Every seven sets of seven years brought Jubilee, which was a year of complete restoration and freedom. This isn't coincidence, it's intentional design. The pattern of seven reveals that rest and renewal aren't afterthoughts in God's economy; they're central to how He intended life to function.

This pattern even extends to the culmination of all things. Hebrews chapter four speaks of a final Sabbath rest that remains for God's people—an eternal encore where what was begun in creation reaches its ultimate fulfillment.

When we understand Sabbath as God's encore, it transforms how we approach it. No longer is it an obligation to fulfill but a gift to unwrap. Not a restriction to endure but an invitation to wonder. Not just a cessation of activity but a celebration of presence.

The encore effect teaches us something special about God's heart. He values presence over productivity, communion over constant creation, being with over doing for. And He invites us into this same value system, a completely countercultural approach to time, work, and relationship.

In our achievement-oriented world, stopping can feel like failure. But in God's economy, the sacred pause isn't weakness but wisdom. It's not avoidance of responsibility but the foundation for meaningful engagement with it.

The encore reminds us that sometimes the most meaningful moment isn't found in creating more but in savoring what already exists. Not in doing one more thing, but in being fully present to what has been done.

This is exactly what God did with Sabbath. He wrote a sacred rest into the score of creation, knowing that without this deliberate pause, the full beauty of what He had made couldn't be fully appreciated or experienced.

Does your breathless pace of projects, presentations, errands, schedules and achievements need the counterbalance of sacred pause?

The invitation to Sabbath is God's encore. His masterful conclusion that gives meaning to everything. This invitation becomes even more meaningful when we consider that He designed it with you in mind.

Designed With You In Mind

Life brings seasons of challenge. Sometimes gentle rain, sometimes fierce tempests. Perhaps you're weathering one right now, or perhaps you can see clouds gathering on your horizon. We all face storms at various points in our journey.

While acknowledging life's storms might not initially feel encouraging, understanding who God is and what He's provided can radically change how you navigate these waters. This is where Sabbath becomes not just a nice ritual but a life-preserving necessity.

God saw this coming. He knew that in our human frailty, we would tend toward overloading our schedules and overestimating our capabilities. He knew we would need not just physical rest but spiritual reconnection—time set apart to remember who we are before addressing what we do.

God didn't create Sabbath because we needed a break from work; He created it because we needed regular, rhythmic reconnection with Him. It's less about ceasing activity and more about entering His presence.

Sabbath is designed with you in mind.

I'll never forget last year on Michael's birthday when I was desperately searching for the perfect gift. (You know that panic when you want to find something that says 'I really know you and love you' but everything in the store screams 'last-minute shopping'?) After wandering through countless stores and scrolling websites, I finally had a lightbulb moment: I'd make him something completely unique—a shirt featuring all his race cities and bringing to mind so many of our special family memories.

When he unwrapped it, the look of pure joy on his face reminded me what gift-giving is really about. It's not just the item; it's the love and intention behind it.

That's the heart behind Sabbath. It's a gift that's been waiting since creation for you to unwrap it. And unlike most gifts, this one gets better with each week you open it.

"Look, God has given you the Sabbath." (Exodus 16:29 NIV)

These words were spoken to the Israelites in the wilderness, a mixed multitude of people who had just escaped slavery. Remarkably, God gave this Sabbath instruction before they even reached Mount Sinai, before the Ten Commandments were formalized, showing that Sabbath was a gift offered before it became a commandment. The invitation wasn't just for the Jews, but for everyone who came out of Egypt with them: people from various nations and backgrounds who joined in the exodus.

Put yourself in their sandals for a moment. For generations, their worth had been measured solely by their productivity. Their entire existence had been defined by making bricks, meeting quotas, proving their value through endless work. Their bodies bore the scars of a system that saw them only as units of production.

And now, this God of liberation was telling them something revolutionary: **You are more than what you produce. Your value isn't found in your output. Your worth isn't measured by your usefulness. You are precious to Me because I created you for relationship.**

God wasn't imposing another burden; He was offering freedom to all who would receive it. He was rewriting their identity from "slave" to "beloved."

This gift wasn't exclusive to one group but was meant for all of humanity. From the very beginning, Sabbath was meant to be a blessing for everyone regardless of nationality, social standing, or spiritual heritage. What a revolutionary concept in ancient times and perhaps even more radical in our culture today.

The invitation to Sabbath isn't a new spiritual discipline to master but a return to the original design. This gift has been sitting wrapped on your doorstep since the beginning of time. Not hidden away, but placed in plain sight at the very beginning of Scripture—the divine pause button your exhausted heart has been desperately searching for.

What if the transformation you've been struggling to manufacture through more effort, more discipline, more striving has been waiting all along in the weekly rhythm of sacred rest?

The gift has been sitting wrapped on your doorstep since the beginning of time.

But how did Jesus, the Lord of the Sabbath, show us how to unwrap it?

A BREAK
RESTORES
YOUR ENERGY
SABBATH

REVEALS

YOUR
IDENTITY

Chapter Seven

At the Table with Jesus

When we examine Jesus's relationship with Sabbath, we discover something revolutionary. Jesus removed the legalistic distortions and restored its life-giving essence. His approach transforms our understanding of Sabbath from religious obligation to divine relationship—from rule-keeping to soul restoration.

> "Do not think that I have come to abolish the Law or the Prophets; I have not come to abolish them but to fulfill them" (Matthew 5:17 NIV).

These words reveal Jesus' relationship to all of Scripture, including the Sabbath commandment. He didn't come to discard sacred rhythms established since creation, but to reveal their deepest purpose and restore their original intent.

The Gospels record at least seven significant Sabbath encounters where Jesus intentionally challenged misunderstandings about this divine gift. In each instance, He wasn't dismissing Sabbath—He was revealing its true purpose.

What's fascinating is learning that Jesus regularly attended synagogue on the Sabbath "as was his custom" (Luke 4:16). This brief detail provides a remarkable glimpse into Jesus' regular spiritual practice before His public ministry. Though Scripture tells us relatively little about Jesus' life before age thirty, this glimpse reveals He placed a priority on Sabbath observance.

Jesus embraced the Sabbath as an essential rhythm of His own spiritual life.

Even more significantly, Jesus chose the Sabbath for His first public teaching. In Luke's account, Jesus stands in the synagogue, unrolls the scroll of Isaiah, and reads:

> "The Spirit of the Lord is on me, because he has anointed me to proclaim good news to the poor. He has sent me to proclaim freedom for the prisoners and recovery of sight for the blind, to set the oppressed free, to proclaim the year of the Lord's favor" (Luke 4:18-19 NIV).

Then, with every eye fastened on him, Jesus makes the astonishing declaration: "Today this scripture is fulfilled in your hearing" (Luke 4:21 NIV).

This wasn't a random choice of timing. By deliberately selecting Sabbath for this inaugural message, Jesus was establishing an important connection. The liberty, healing, and restoration He came to bring aligned perfectly with Sabbath's original purpose. In this moment, Jesus was declaring that He himself was the fulfillment of Sabbath's deepest meaning.

From Rules to Relationship

The religious leaders of Jesus' day had transformed Sabbath from a gift into a burden. What began as a divine invitation to rest had become an anxious obligation governed by hundreds of detailed restrictions.

By the first century, Sabbath observance included 39 categories of forbidden activities, each with numerous sub-rules and exceptions. The gift had been buried under layers of human regulation.

Into this context, Jesus spoke some of his most liberating words: "The Sabbath was made for man, not man for the Sabbath." (Mark 2:27 NIV).

With this simple statement, Jesus completely inverted the prevailing understanding. He reclaimed its true purpose—to benefit humanity, not to burden it. To restore rather than restrict. To liberate rather than limit.

Jesus consistently demonstrated this understanding through his actions. When his disciples plucked grain on the Sabbath because they were hungry, he defended them against accusations of Sabbath-breaking (Matthew 12:1-8). When he encountered people suffering on the Sabbath, he healed them without hesitation:

> A man with a withered hand in the synagogue (Matthew 12:9-14)

> A woman bent double for eighteen years (Luke 13:10-17)

> A man born blind (John 9:1-16)

> A man with dropsy (Luke 14:1-6)

With each healing, Jesus revealed Sabbath's true character. "Is it lawful to do good on the Sabbath?" he asked the religious leaders, exposing the absurdity of a Sabbath interpretation that would prevent acts of compassion and restoration.

Jesus wasn't breaking the Sabbath; he was breaking its misinterpretation. He wasn't dismissing the commandment; he was demonstrating its fulfillment through relationship rather than regulation.

This perspective transforms our approach to Sabbath entirely. No longer is it primarily about what we cannot do but about Who we can commune with. Not a list of prohibitions but an invitation to presence. Not religious performance but divine relationship.

In our first attempts at establishing a Sabbath rhythm, we felt the same tension. We worried about getting 'it right.' What foods we should make, what words should be spoken. The breakthrough came when we realized we were focusing on the wrong thing. We were perfecting the form rather than experiencing the relationship.

Sabbath isn't about adherence to rules but about regular reconnection with the Ruler of all creation.

Rather than dismantling Sabbath, Jesus restored it to its original design. He wanted his followers to experience the full blessing of Sabbath as it was intended:

> To experience the blessing of rest and spiritual renewal

> To reconnect with our Creator and the world He made

> To remember the covenant God made with His people

> A time to remember your redemption and all that God has done

These four purposes transcend any particular tradition or cultural expression. The form may vary, but the posture of the heart is what matters.

The Source of True Rest

In the middle of Jesus' ministry, he extends this remarkable invitation:

"Come to me, all you who are weary and burdened, and I will give you rest. Take my yoke upon you and learn from me, for I am gentle and humble in heart, and you will find rest for your souls.

For my yoke is easy and my burden is light"
(Matthew 11:28-30 NIV).

These words reveal something profound about Jesus' self-understanding and mission. He didn't just teach about rest; He presented Himself as its source. He didn't merely offer techniques for managing stress; He invited people into His presence as the ultimate restoration.

When Jesus declared, "The Son of Man is Lord of the Sabbath" (Matthew 12:8 NIV), He was making an extraordinary claim. In Jewish understanding, Sabbath was God's institution—established at creation, reinforced at Sinai. By claiming lordship over Sabbath, Jesus was asserting His divine authority, placing Himself in the position of the One who had instituted Sabbath in the first place.

This wasn't just a theological statement but a practical invitation. As Lord of Sabbath, Jesus was redefining it, not as the absence of activity but as the presence of relationship with Him.

The metaphor of the yoke is particularly powerful. A yoke was a wooden frame that connected two oxen for pulling a load, typically a younger, inexperienced animal paired with an older, stronger one that would bear the bulk of the weight and set the pace. Jesus invites us into this kind of partnership to walk alongside Him, learning from His gentleness, finding that what seemed like an impossible burden becomes manageable in His presence.

This redefines rest entirely. It's not just cessation of activity but partnership with the Prince of Peace. Not just taking a break but entering a relationship. Not just recovery from exhaustion but realignment with our design through communion with our Designer.

While rest can be found partly through setting boundaries, disconnecting technology, or enjoying nature, ultimate rest is found only in relationship with the Source of rest Himself. Jesus doesn't just offer rest as a concept or practice; He embodies it and invites us to find it in Him.

Throughout His ministry, Jesus modeled this understanding of true rest. The Gospels frequently mention Him retreating to solitary places to pray (Luke 5:16), withdrawing with His disciples for rest (Mark 6:31), seeking communion with the Father apart from the demands of ministry.

This wasn't self-indulgence or avoidance of responsibility. It was strategic renewal. A reconnection with His source that empowered His service. Jesus didn't rest instead of fulfilling His mission; He rested in order to fulfill it with greater clarity, compassion, and power.

Here we see the Sabbath Soul Cycle in perfect action—pressing pause to find rest, which leads to renewed delight in His calling, which activates purpose that transforms the world. The rhythm doesn't end with rest; it overflows into mission.

A Foretaste of Eternity

Jesus' approach to Sabbath points us toward something even greater: a future reality where our rest will be complete.

Isaiah prophesies that Sabbath won't disappear in eternity; it will be fully realized: "From one Sabbath to another, all mankind will come and bow down before me, says the LORD" (Isaiah 66:23 NIV).

This scripture reveals that Sabbath is not a temporary practice for our earthly journey but a glimpse of our eternal destination. It's both present discipline and prophetic sign, a foretaste of the ultimate rest we were created for.

The writer of Hebrews makes this connection: "There remains, then, a Sabbath-rest for the people of God; for anyone who enters God's rest also rests from their works, just as God did from his" (Hebrews 4:9-10

NIV). This passage connects the weekly Sabbath with a greater, more comprehensive rest that awaits God's people—an eternal communion with the Creator unhindered by sin, striving, or separation.

Every Sabbath we observe now is a prophetic act that points to this future reality—the day when all creation will be restored, when striving will cease, when communion with God will be unbroken and unhindered.

I experienced this profound truth during a particularly difficult season in our lives. Every Friday evening, as we entered Sabbath time, something remarkable happened. It wasn't that our problems disappeared (they were still very much present) but our perspective shifted dramatically.

For those sacred hours, we experienced a peace that truly transcended understanding. Not because our circumstances had changed, but because Sabbath allowed us to step momentarily into a different reality—one governed not by urgent problems but by eternal promises, not by pressing deadlines but by God's perfect timing.

It was as if Sabbath blurs the lines where heaven and earth collide, where we taste the peace of eternity even in the midst of temporal turmoil. We experience what theologians call the "already but not yet"—the paradox of Christian existence where the future kingdom breaks into present reality, where eternal peace infuses temporal chaos.

Sabbath is prophetic participation in the eternal reality that awaits us. It's rehearsal for eternity.

When viewed through this lens, Sabbath becomes not just a nice spiritual discipline but a necessary alignment with ultimate reality. It's not just taking a break from the temporal but touching the eternal. Not just ceasing activity but entering presence.

From Obligation to Relationship

Jesus' approach to Sabbath reveals the heart of His entire ministry. His mission was bringing us into living relationship. Every aspect of His interaction with Sabbath reveals this central purpose:

> He honored the practice while liberating it from legalism

> He fulfilled its deepest meaning through His presence and work

> He revealed Himself as the source of true rest

> He connected it to the eternal reality we await

When we understand Jesus as the Lord of Sabbath, we discover a perspective shift with how we approach our weekly practice. We're no longer asking, "Am I doing this right?" but "Am I creating space for relationship?" Not "Have I followed all the rules?" but "Have I encountered the Ruler of all?" Not "Have I properly rested?" but "Have I deeply connected with the Source of rest?"

The invitation stands before you. Not to religious observance but to relationship with the One who designed rest as the pathway to your flourishing.

Will you accept His invitation to find rest not in a day but in God? To experience not just the shadow of rest but its very substance in Jesus Christ? This is the fulfillment of Sabbath: not its end, but its ultimate expression in relationship with the One who created it for your good and His glory.

But how do you actually start Sabbath? How do you translate this wisdom into modern practice?

The answer is simpler than you think.

most good things
start

AWKWARDLY.
START
ANYWAY

CHAPTER EIGHT

Simple Steps to Start

"So what exactly do you *do* during Sabbath?"

It's the question we get most often, usually accompanied by a mix of curiosity and apprehension. I get it.The concept sounds appealing in theory, but how does it actually work in real life?

Let's move from the why of Sabbath to the what, translating this wisdom into practical application for modern life. How do we engage in this sacred communion with God in the 21st century, amid soccer practices and work deadlines and the constant ping of notifications?

First, let me ease your mind: there's no single "right way" to practice Sabbath. These aren't rigid rules but flexible frameworks that create space for the sacred to enter your ordinary routines. **We've discovered that authenticity isn't found in perfect replication of someone else's tradition; it's found in genuine connection with God and each other.**

The question isn't "Am I doing this right?" but rather "Is this creating space for God's presence?"

Our goal is to keep God at the center and draw closer to His heart. As we do this, the Bible promises that He will move closer to us, and we will be connected closer to each other. As James 4:8 reminds us, "Come near to God and he will come near to you" (NIV).

Signaling Sabbath

Remember Christmas morning as a child, that magical anticipation, heart racing with excitement for what awaits? The way time seemed to stretch out before the big day, each moment laden with possibility? There's something almost electric about that sense of anticipation: knowing something special is about to happen.

That's exactly what begins to happen as Sabbath takes root in your life.

There's a moment when Sabbath transforms from something you do to something you hold within you. In the days and hours leading up to Sabbath, your being begins to "Signal Sabbath" knowing that something sacred is approaching, not just in your calendar, but in your heart. Like that Christmas morning flutter, the anticipation becomes tangible; but instead of waiting for gifts under a tree, you're anticipating communion with your Creator.

> Your **THINKING** shifts from "What needs to get done?" to "What can I share that honors what Jesus has done in my life this week?"

> Your **TALKING** becomes more intentional, conversations with family members throughout the week take on deeper meaning as you notice moments worth celebrating.

> Your **ACTIONS** become purposeful, from grocery shopping with intention to planning the meal with thoughtfulness, because Jesus is at the table with you.

God loves when we come expectant. Anticipation is a form of worship. This isn't just dinner prep—it's soul and spirit prep.

Sabbath State of Mind

Before anything else, Sabbath begins with a heart shift. This moves us from doing to being. This isn't just another activity; it's creating a sacred moment.

For me, this means finding a few minutes of quiet before our Sabbath begins. I'll take one last check of emails and texts (not to respond, just to acknowledge), jot down anything urgent that I'll need to address after Sabbath, and then here's the crucial part: **I turn my phone completely off.**

Not silent. Not Do Not Disturb. **Off.**

This simple act is revolutionary in our always-connected world. The first time I did it, I felt actual physical anxiety, like I was cutting off a vital organ. But then a wave of relief washed over me. For the next few hours, I wasn't responsible for solving anyone's problems outside my immediate family. I was free, truly free, to be fully present where I was.

It's my way of saying to God, "The next handful of hours are yours. Nothing else is more important."

Modern technology actually makes this disconnect easier than ever. Use your device's 'Focus' mode, 'Do Not Disturb' settings, or built-in Sabbath features. This technology-free zone in your week might be the most compelling invitation to something deeper.

I take a few deep breaths and mentally prepare to receive rather than achieve. The goal is to shift gears—from productive to present.

As I get ready to take a seat at the table, I often prayerfully read these verses from Isaiah:

> "Keep the Sabbath day holy. Don't pursue your own interests on that day, but enjoy the Sabbath and speak of it with delight as the Lord's holy day. Honor the Sabbath in everything you do on that day, and don't follow your own desires or talk idly. Then the Lord will be your delight. I will give you great honor and satisfy you with the inheritance I promised to your ancestor Jacob. I, the Lord, have spoken!" (Isaiah 58:13-14 NLT).

This mental preparation creates fertile soil for everything that follows. Just as an athlete visualizes success before stepping onto the field, this intentional heart-centering prepares you to fully receive the gift that awaits.

It's the threshold between the ordinary and the sacred. The moment where true transformation begins.

Setting the Space

The physical environment shapes our internal experience more than we realize. Setting the space for Sabbath isn't about creating Instagram-worthy tablescapes. **It's about simple touches that signal "this is more than dinner, this is something special."**

In our home, we have a few items reserved exclusively for Sabbath: a beautiful wooden board for our bread, special glasses for the juice, and two candles at the center of the table. We typically bring out nicer dishes, though we've certainly had seasons when life demanded simplicity.

One practical tradition that helps our family transition into Sabbath time is preparing a simple charcuterie board with fruit, veggies, cheese, nuts, and crackers. It brings me joy to see the colors and textures of our creative God on display. It's like creating an edible canvas that reflects the beauty of God's creation.

When everyone is seated, we take a collective breath and say *"Shabbat Shalom"* together. This encompasses "Sabbath Wholeness Peace". This meaning is more than the absence of conflict, but shalom is a whole peace in spirit, mind, and body. It's the difference between feeling rested after a good night's sleep and experiencing wholeness in every fiber of your being. This greeting marks the threshold moment when ordinary time becomes sacred time, and we enter a space designed for restoration. What we discovered is that our ordinary dining table becomes an altar. A sacred space where heaven touches earth, where our family can come just as we are.

Unlike sitting side by side on a couch facing a screen, a table positions us face-to-face. We can see each other's expressions, make eye contact, truly engage. There's something primal about breaking bread together that transcends cultural boundaries and speaks to our shared humanity.

Remember that Sabbath welcomes our full humanity—tears, frustrations, and all. There will be evenings when someone is upset or when family tensions are simmering. In those moments, everything in you will want to abandon the practice, thinking, "This isn't working." **Take another deep breath and continue anyway.** Often these "messy" Sabbaths speak most loudly to your family. They demonstrate that this invitation isn't about perfection but about presence. It's about showing up exactly as we are and creating space for God to meet us there.

Steps to Sabbath

Now let's explore the core elements of our Sabbath experience. We'll review the simple flow that transforms chaos into peace. These four easy steps create the framework for our evening each Friday night. And here's the best part: the entire sequence takes about 15 minutes but with infinitely more lasting impact. Our journey led us to this particular practice, but yours may look different. That's the beauty of Sabbath is that it can be authentically expressed in ways that resonate with your unique family and circumstances while capturing the heart of sacred rest.

The Devotional

First, we begin by inviting God to the table with a time of sharing.

This is an opportunity to share a brief devotional—perhaps a scripture that spoke to you during the week, a reflection on current events through God's lens, or sharing something you noticed God doing in your family.

Consider beginning with Psalm 92, known as 'A Psalm for the Sabbath Day'—this psalm declares: 'It is good to praise the LORD and make music to your name, O Most High, proclaiming your love in the morning and your faithfulness at night' (Psalm 92:1-2). Reading this psalm helps sanctify the day, setting it apart as holy just as God intended.

But here's what transforms this from a monologue to a dialogue: invite each family member to bring something to share. Encourage your children throughout the week to notice:

> A way they saw Jesus in their life

> Something from their Bible reading or devotions

> A word of encouragement for the family

> A flower, a drawing, or any expression of wonder

When both parents and children participate in welcoming God, it elevates everyone's heart and demonstrates that Sabbath belongs to the whole family, not just the adults.

This doesn't need elaborate preparation—authenticity matters more than eloquence. The goal is creating space where God feels welcomed and everyone feels invited to participate.

This starting moment sets the tone for the entire evening. It's our way of acknowledging God's power and presence, inviting Him to be the honored guest at our table. Some weeks it's deeply moving; other weeks it's simple. But it always centers us on the true purpose of our gathering—not just family time, but sacred communion with God and each other.

The Candles

Second, the lighting of the candles symbolizes bringing God's light into our home and hearts.

Have you noticed how candlelight changes a space? How it softens harsh edges and creates an atmosphere of warmth? How it draws everyone's attention to its gentle flicker? A little bit of light dispels a lot of darkness.

One of God's first acts when He began to turn chaos into peace was to speak on day 1 and say, "Let there be light" (Genesis 1:3). Interestingly, this light came before the sun, moon, and stars were even created on day four, pointing to a divine light that transcends our physical understanding. Scripture tells us that in the New Jerusalem, "There will be no more night. They will not need the light of a lamp or the light of the sun, for the Lord God will give them light" (Revelation 22:5 NIV).

There's something special about candlelight. Whether it's a candle on a birthday cake, a votive on a table at a romantic evening, or a Roman candle on the 4th of July, flames capture our attention and signal that something special is happening.

For our family, the lighting of the candles reminds us that this time is not just another dinner, but we're expectant to see what the Lord of Sabbath has in store for us today. Most Sabbath dinners, we use two candles just like in Jewish tradition, though sometimes we've used one, three, or even enjoyed a candlelight lit mealtime.

As we light the candles, we take a moment to welcome the presence of God. We've adapted this moment to acknowledge God's presence illuminating our darkness.

The Blessing

Third comes what might be the most treasured part of our Sabbath experience. We take time to speak a blessing over each family member and guest.

Throughout the week, Michael jots down moments when he notices something special about each family member. Then, during our Sabbath time of blessing, he shares these observations one by one. "Nya, I noticed how patient you were with your little brother when he was having a hard time." "Anchor, I saw your generosity when you shared your treat without being asked."

These aren't generic compliments but specific affirmations that reflect the unique image of God we see in each person. They're not based on performance or achievement but on character and essence—who they are, not just what they've done.

There's also a beautiful moment where I, as the husband, intentionally honor Selah before the family, drawing inspiration from Proverbs 31. In a culture that often undermines marriage, this public affirmation speaks volumes to our children about the value and sanctity of our covenant relationship.

> "A wife of noble character who can find? She is worth far more than rubies" (Proverbs 31:10 NIV).

When I look into Selah's eyes and tell her specifically what I've seen in her that reflects God's character (her strength, wisdom, kindness, or faith), something sacred happens that strengthens the very foundation of our covenant. It's not flattery but recognition. I'm seeing and naming the divine image in my spouse.

There's something powerful about looking someone in the eyes and speaking words of life and destiny over them.

We then all join in and say the Priestly Blessing from Numbers 6:24-26 together: "The Lord bless you and keep you; the Lord make his face shine on you and be gracious to you; the Lord turn his face toward you and give you peace" (NIV).

These sacred words, spoken over God's people for thousands of years, remind us that we are recipients of divine blessing. They invoke God's protection, favor, grace, and peace, not because we've earned it, but because of His faithful character.

The Cup and Bread

Finally, we share communion, connecting our Sabbath experience to remembering what Jesus did for us.

On the night before His crucifixion, Jesus took bread and wine with His disciples and established this remembrance. "This is my body given for you; do this in remembrance of me... This cup is the new covenant in my blood, which is poured out for you" (Luke 22:19-20 NIV).

By incorporating communion into our weekly rhythm, we're both remembering Jesus' sacrifice and inviting His presence into our present moment. We're acknowledging that our Sabbath rest is made possible by His finished work.

We bless the cup: "Blessed are you, Lord our God, King of the universe, who creates the fruit of the vine."

Our family likes to collectively say "to life!" as we all lift our glasses.

We bless the bread: "Blessed are you, Lord our God, King of the universe, who brings forth bread from the earth."

Then we enjoy our meal together, without rushing, often using conversation starters to deepen our connection.

The physical elements of bread and juice (or wine, depending on your tradition) engage our senses in the experience. We taste, touch, see, and smell these elements that connect us not only to Jesus's last meal with his disciples but to thousands of years of God's people gathering around tables to remember His goodness.

Jesus sets an example for all of us on how to keep our spirit and soul aligned to what is most important. Him!

Get Lost in the Linger

We love how our friends say, 'We don't rush back to the world. We linger in the peace.'

In a world addicted to acceleration, there's something revolutionary about lingering. Those who master the art of unhurried presence discover what the constantly rushing miss entirely: the divine whispers, the sacred connections, the unexpected inspirations that arrive only when we create space for them. **This isn't just slowing down, it's tuning into a frequency drowned out by hurry.**

After the formal elements of our Sabbath—the candles, prayers, blessings, and communion—comes what might be the most cherished aspect of the entire practice: the unhurried presence we call "the linger."

No rushing to clean up. No checking phones for missed messages. No hurrying to the next activity. Just being fully present together without agenda or time constraints. Conversation flows naturally. Laughter emerges spontaneously. Connection deepens without effort.

For high-achievers like us, this aspect of Sabbath presented a particular challenge. Michael is naturally oriented toward action and impact. And I'm wired for efficiency. The invitation to simply linger without agenda felt very abnormal.

Yet we discovered that this seemingly "unproductive" time often yields the richest moments of connection and insight—precisely because it's not forced or scheduled. When we remove the pressure to produce and perform, something beautiful emerges naturally in the space created.

Carrying the Light

The threshold works both ways. Just as you intentionally entered Sabbath space, be mindful of how you carry its gifts back into daily life.

The world has been spinning while you've been replenishing. Notice what you now hold that those around you desperately need:

> More patience from experiencing unhurried presence

> Deeper peace from communion with God

> Greater joy from authentic connection

> Renewed perspective from stepping outside time's pressure

Your family, friends, and colleagues will encounter someone different. Not because you're trying to be different, but because you've been filled.

We are called to be lights to the world. When we carry peace and wholeness into ordinary moments, we transform them simply by showing up differently. **This is how Sabbath multiplies—changing the hours you set apart, and influencing the hours that follow.**

Start Where You Are

If all of this feels overwhelming, let me suggest the simplest way to begin: This Friday, turn off your phones. Light a candle. Say a blessing over each person at your table. That's it.

Don't wait for the perfect week or the ideal circumstances. This Friday evening press pause and tune into being present. That's all it takes to start Sabbath.

The table is set. The invitation is extended. The decision is yours. Will you pull up a seat?

Once you do, you'll find how fun it is to make this beautiful practice authentically yours.

FIFTY-TWO OPPORTUNITIES TO SPEAK LIFE

into those you love.

CHAPTER NINE

Making It Yours

You'll quickly discover this practice isn't one-size-fits-all. The beauty of Sabbath is how it adapts to your unique circumstances, personality, and season of life while maintaining its transformative essence.

We needed to make Sabbath our own. To find the balance between honoring the ancient wisdom and creating something authentic for our family, in our particular time and place.

The beauty of this sacred invitation is that while the purpose of creating space for God's presence and genuine connection remains constant, the form can flex to fit your specific season and needs. **Whether you're single or married, have young children or are empty nesters, live a structured life or are navigating unpredictable schedules, the transformative power of Sabbath is available to you.**

Let's explore how to make Sabbath authentically yours, not by mimicking someone else's tradition, but by capturing your personal expression that will create family traditions lasting generations.

The Blessing: The Superpower of Sabbath

We've discovered one element that consistently transforms families more than any other: the blessing. (you're gonna love this!)

Think about it. where else in our culture do we regularly speak intentional words of life and affirmation over those we love? This is your opportunity to do this 52 times a year!

When was the last time someone looked you in the eyes and spoke specific words of blessing over you? Not generic praise for something you'd accomplished, but words that recognized and affirmed your inherent worth, your unique gifts, your sacred identity? For most of us, such moments are rare and precious.

There's profound power in these moments of focused affirmation. When we look someone directly in the eyes and speak specific words of blessing over them, something extraordinary happens. The barriers that we so carefully maintain throughout the week begin to dissolve. The soil of the heart becomes receptive to truth in a way that's rare in our distracted, defensive daily lives.

Through these blessings, we not only affirm who someone is now but help them discover deeper aspects of their God-given identity. We're essentially holding up a mirror that reflects not just their current self but their potential in Christ. Each blessing becomes another brushstroke in the masterpiece God is painting of their   true self.

The practice of blessing others transforms not just the receiver but the giver as well.

It develops what we might call a "blessing radar": an awareness throughout the week that causes you to notice and catalog the beautiful qualities in those around you. You begin watching for moments of courage, kindness, wisdom, and growth in your spouse, your children, your friends. Your perspective shifts from problem-spotting to treasure-hunting.

I notice this shift in my own thinking as Friday approaches. Throughout the week, I find myself mentally noting moments to mention during our blessing time: how a family member handled a difficult conversation with patience, helped someone without being asked, or showed creativity in solving a problem. This awareness itself is transformational—it reorients my attention toward the beauty in those I love rather than their flaws or failings.

This shift is desperately needed in a world saturated with criticism and comparison.

The battlefield of the mind is littered with negative self-talk, doubt, and depreciation. Our internal narratives often default to what we've done wrong, where we've fallen short, how we don't measure up. The blessing element of Sabbath directly counters this destructive pattern by consistently reminding us and those we love of the divine image we bear, the unique gifts we carry, the specific ways we reflect God's character.

The impact is compounding. Week after week, these truths begin to sink deeper, gradually rewriting the internal scripts that have played for years. We've watched our children's confidence grow, not in arrogance but in a secure knowledge of Who they are and Whose they are.

We've watched our marriage flourish as these weekly blessings create a foundation of mutual appreciation and admiration, acting as a protective barrier against the inevitable stresses that threaten to erode intimacy. In a world that often focuses on what's wrong with our spouse, this practice trains us to consistently articulate what's right.

Sometimes the kids get so caught up in the spirit of blessing that they take turns blessing Michael after the blessing is extended to them. **There's an overflow of abundance when the giver becomes the receiver because the power of reciprocation takes over.** These moments often bring tears to my eyes—watching our children internalize and then express this language of affirmation reveals the deep work God is doing in their hearts.

I'll never forget the night our youngest daughter, just seven at the time, placed her hands on my shoulders and declared with complete seriousness, "I bless you because you are brave and strong and you love Jesus." The simplicity and sincerity of her words touched something deep in all of us. She wasn't merely mimicking what she'd heard; she was participating in a sacred exchange that transcended her years.

This consistent practice of blessing has transformed our family culture in lasting ways. It creates a foundation of security and affirmation that our children carry with them throughout the week. The words spoken at the Sabbath table become reminders of truth when lies threaten to overwhelm.

"It takes maybe fifteen seconds," a mother of three told us, eyes glistening. "Just fifteen seconds of my husband speaking blessing over each of us. But those few words echo through our home all week long." Her husband nodded. "I spent years climbing corporate ladders. But nothing, and I mean nothing, has shaped my family like looking my children in the eyes every week and declaring who they truly are."

In a culture where genuine eye contact and focused attention have become increasingly rare, the blessing creates a sacred space for connection at the soul level. It says, "I see you—not just your performance or behavior, but the essence of who you are. And what I see is beautiful, valuable, and loved."

Fifty-two opportunities each year to speak life.

Fifty-two chances to counter the world's criticism with specific, intentional affirmation.

Fifty-two sacred moments to participate in God's ongoing work of forming identity and purpose in those entrusted to our care.

We believe the power of blessing is Sabbath's best-kept secret, and it's exactly what our wounded world desperately needs. Now comes the exciting part—making this world-changing practice authentically yours!

Finding Your Sabbath Style

Around the world and across different traditions, families practice Sabbath in ways that reflect their unique cultures and circumstances. Some homes celebrate with formal attire and elaborate meals prepared in advance. Others gather around simple food and casual settings. Some follow traditional liturgies while others create contemporary expressions. Yet in each, the unmistakable presence of the sacred can be felt—not because of the form, but because of the intention to meet with God.

What makes Sabbath beautiful is how it adapts to and enhances the unique dynamics of each family. In our home, we've watched with wonder as each family member has found their own way to participate and contribute to this sacred time.

One tradition that has brought unexpected joy is letting each child take turns choosing a special Sabbath snack or dessert for the family. **There's something powerful about giving children ownership in creating the sacred moments they'll remember forever.** Whether it's homemade cookies, fresh fruit arranged in a beautiful pattern, or a simple bowl of popcorn for sharing, when children contribute to the preparation, they're not just participating—they're investing. We've watched our kids beam with pride as they present their chosen treat, explaining why they picked it and how they want to share it. These small acts of hospitality teach them that Sabbath belongs to them too, that they have a voice in shaping our family's sacred traditions. **The snack itself matters far less than the sense of ownership and anticipation it creates. This gives our children a way to move from passive participants into active contributors.**

These personal expressions show how Sabbath has integrated into our family identity—not as an imposed ritual but as a living tradition that each person makes their own.

As you consider what Sabbath might look like in your context, here are some variations to consider:

For Singles

If you're single, consider hosting a Sabbath dinner for friends, or create a personal Sabbath ritual that includes elements meaningful to you like hiking, journaling, or creating art. The rhythm of communing with God is the constant, and in the sacred space of singleness, you have the unique gift of undivided attention to hear His heart for yours.

For Empty Nesters

As children grow and leave home, Sabbath can evolve. Many empty nesters find this is a perfect time to extend hospitality, inviting others to their Sabbath table. It can also become a beautiful way to nurture ongoing connections with grown children and create special traditions with grandchildren.

For Families with Young Children

Sabbath offers a powerful opportunity for spiritual formation. This is a time for intentionally passing your values and faith to the next generation through meaningful participation and giving them ownership in your family's faith journey. When children participate in meaningful ways, they don't just observe traditions—they embody them.

For Working Professionals

As leaders ourselves, we understand the unique pressures that come with demanding schedules. For professionals who can't observe

Friday evenings, honoring the spirit of Sabbath matters more than the specific day.

Paul affirms this principle in Romans 14:5: 'One person considers one day more sacred than another; another considers every day alike. Each of them should be fully convinced in their own mind' (NIV). The key is consistency and intentionality—a time reserved to review God's faithfulness in the week behind us and invite His presence into the week ahead of you.

Marveling at What the Table Brings Out

We've been amazed at how our Sabbath table has brought out unique aspects in each of our children, qualities and gifts that might have remained dormant in the rush of everyday life.

Nya has found her gift in her melodic voice and loves singing the *Shema* a cappella: the ancient prayer from Deuteronomy 6 that Jesus himself would have memorized and recited as a child. The first time she volunteered to lead this sacred declaration of faith, we were stunned by the confidence and reverence in her young voice. Something about the safety of our Sabbath circle gave her courage to step into this gift, connecting her to thousands of years of faithful children who have spoken these same words. Now it's become her special contribution to our practice.

Tinsley loves to perform a worship dance after dinner, which sometimes turns into a full family dance party with everyone joining in. There's a freedom and joy that emerges in these moments that feels different from the ordinary. Her natural expressiveness flourishes in this sacred space. The first time she was nervous—peeking around the corner with excitement and hesitation. "I made up a dance to show God how I love Him," she whispered. As the music began, her self-consciousness melted away into movements that were full of worship.

One Friday evening, our son Anchor beat everyone to the table and exclaimed, "I've been waiting for this all week!" Not because we were having a special meal or friends were joining us or there was a celebration planned, but simply because he had begun to crave the sacred space we created together each week.

Watching him there, eyes bright with anticipation for our family's sacred time, I realized we were witnessing the fulfillment of God's multigenerational vision described in Psalms 78: "He decreed statutes for Jacob and established the law in Israel, which he commanded our ancestors to teach their children, so the next generation would know them, even the children yet to be born, and they in turn would tell their children. Then they would put their trust in God and would not forget his deeds but would keep his commands" (Psalm 78:5-7 NIV).

Without a single lecture about the importance of spiritual disciplines, Anchor had caught something we couldn't have taught him directly: a hunger for God's presence, a desire for family connection, a recognition of the sacred in the midst of ordinary life. The table was becoming his inheritance, a place where faith was being absorbed rather than imposed.

It was a moment of gratitude for me, a glimpse of how this beautiful practice was reshaping not just our schedules, but our desires. The transformation wasn't happening through force or obligation, but through the gentle power of consistent rhythm that would echo far beyond our generation.

This multigenerational impact extends beyond our own family.

We've also witnessed how Sabbath has impacted other families who have shared the experience with us. There's something powerful about modeling this practice rather than just talking about it.

Seeing other families incorporate elements into their own rhythm and hearing how it's blessed them has been one of the greatest joys of our journey. **Beyond the core elements we've shared, there's room for your family's unique creativity to flourish.**

Get Creative!

While we've shared the foundational elements of our Sabbath practice, we love to include other creative elements that engage our heart and spirit. There are so many ways to create meaning for you and those you love.

Music: Music moves hearts and sets the atmosphere of Sabbath. We play our "Sabbath Playlist" with a mix of our favorite worship songs and instrumental music. The familiar melodies become part of the ritual, signaling to everyone that we're entering sacred time.

Movement: Going for a walk together, playing a game, doing a puzzle are good ways to rejuvenate your body and mind. Physical activity can be a form of meditation, creating space for connection while keeping restless bodies engaged. Our tradition of a Saturday morning family walk has become as important as the Friday night meal—different in character but equally part of our Sabbath rhythm.

Nature: Connecting with creation by stargazing, sitting by a fire, or watching a sunset can be powerful Sabbath practices. There's something about the vastness of nature that recalibrates our perspective and reminds us of our place in God's grand design. During warmer months, we often move our Sabbath meal outdoors, letting the backdrop of creation enhance our worship.

Creativity: Drawing, writing, or other creative expressions might be your way of tapping into a fresh space with the Creator's presence. Art bypasses our analytical minds and engages our souls directly. One family we know keeps a Sabbath journal where everyone contributes—a drawing, a prayer, a reflection, a poem—creating a beautiful record of their journey together.

Service: Some people incorporate an act of service as part of their Sabbath, finding that giving to others refreshes their own souls. This might seem counterintuitive but service rendered from a place of abundance rather than duty can be deeply rejuvenating. We were inspired to hear of a couple who reserve part of their Sabbath for writing encouraging notes to people who have blessed them that week.

Media: Consider being intentional about any media you consume during Sabbath. Rather than defaulting to whatever's trending, choose films, shows, or music that inspire wonder, promote meaningful conversation, or reflect values you want to cultivate in your family. We occasionally choose a movie that illustrates compassion, courage, or faith, and discuss it afterward.

Hope in the Light

Something stirs in my mother's heart when I watch my children gather around the Sabbath table week after week, their faces illuminated by candlelight, their spirits awakened to the sacred.

Sabbath tradition shapes their spiritual radar for a lifetime.

As our children navigate the complexities of teenage years and young adulthood, my hope is that they'll carry within them a deep knowing—an instinctive ability to discern between spiritual light and darkness because they've experienced both in tangible ways around our table.

The children who grow up with weekly rhythms that welcome God's presence develop an internal compass that recognizes the difference between sacred and ordinary, between divine intimacy and spiritual emptiness. They don't just understand these concepts intellectually; they feel them in their souls.

When they encounter the darkness of this world (the peer pressure, the moral confusion, the spiritual emptiness that characterizes so much of modern culture), something inside them will remember.

They'll reminisce back to those Friday evenings when light pushed back darkness, when peace settled over chaos, when their family chose to step out of the world's frantic pace and into God's presence.

This is the long-term vision we're investing in: raising a generation that instinctively knows the difference between light and darkness, not just as a biblical concept but as a lived reality.

A parent's heart understands deeply that the traditions we establish today become the foundation stones our children will build their lives upon. The weekly rhythm of lighting candles, speaking blessings, and creating sacred space isn't just about this moment; it's about equipping them with spiritual sensitivity for all the moments to come.

When they face crossroads, when they encounter compromise, when the world tries to convince them that all paths lead to the same destination, they'll feel the difference because they've known the light.

Your Sacred Beginning

Remember that your journey will be uniquely yours. Your practice will reflect your family's personality, your specific circumstances, your particular relationship with God.

The beauty of Sabbath is found not in replication but in authentic expression.

This is how your story begins.

PEACE

ISN'T FOUND IN

PERFECT

CIRCUMSTANCES

BUT IN

SACRED
PRESENCE

CHAPTER TEN

Transformation at the Table

When we accept the Sabbath invitation and take our place at the table, something extraordinary begins to unfold. More than just a break from activity, let's zoom out and see the beautiful story that happens when we regularly press pause. These aren't theoretical possibilities but lived realities we've witnessed in our own family and countless others who have embraced this sacred rhythm.

"Does it really matter that much?"

The words escaped my lips before I could catch them. I was standing in our kitchen, disheveled from a day that had gone sideways from the moment I opened my eyes. We were in the middle of one of those weeks (you know the ones) where everything feels like a roller coaster coming off the tracks.

Our youngest had been home sick for three days, alternating between clingy and cranky. My work deadlines had accelerated unexpectedly. Michael had been traveling for work. And then I got an alert that my grocery order for our thoughtfully planned Sabbath dinner was delayed. I couldn't prepare the meal without those ingredients. I was frustrated, stressed, and ready to throw in the towel.

Sabbath was about to begin, and I had nothing prepared. No meal plan. No one had set the table. No energy to design the peaceful atmosphere I desired to create.

Michael took one look at me and responded with a mix of understanding and resolve that I've come to recognize over our years together. He crossed the kitchen to where I stood, placing his hands gently on my shoulders.

"This is exactly why we need Sabbath."

He was right, and I knew it. **The times we most want to skip communion with God are usually the times our souls most desperately need it.**

Peace in the Chaos

That evening, our Sabbath looked different than usual. Quick frozen burgers on the grill. Plastic plates. One candle instead of two, because that's all we could find.

But as we lit that single candle and I watched the flame flicker to life, something shifted in our home. Maybe it was the tangible transition— that cue that said, "Now we pause." Suddenly, I felt all the heaviness I'd been carrying all week begin to lift. The constant mental chatter about deadlines and to-do lists quieted inside me. For the first time in days, I took a full breath, the kind that reaches all the way to fill the bottom of your lungs, and reminds you that you've been shallow-breathing for too long.

This is the first transformation Sabbath brings: peace in the midst of chaos. It doesn't change our circumstances but brings an encounter of the God of peace to them.

The sick child still needed medicine and attention throughout the night. The work deadline was still looming. The house was still cluttered. But something inside me changed. I found my harbor again, my refuge, a sacred space for divine encounter.

Have you noticed how we tend to respond to stress? We either push harder (if one hour of work isn't solving the problem, try two!) or we escape entirely (Netflix binge, anyone?). Neither approach addresses the core issue. One depletes us further; the other merely numbs the symptoms.

Sabbath offers a different way. A deep renewal that doesn't deny reality but transforms how we experience it by bringing us into God's presence.

I'll never forget one Friday night when our daughter Nya looked up, her face glowing, and said ever so simply, "This is what peace feels like." Not a child's superficial happiness but a recognition of something her soul needed and had found. **Out of her mouth came the truth we'd been discovering—that peace isn't found in perfect circumstances but in sacred presence with our Creator.**

Hearts Wide Open

The second transformation appears more gradually: deeper connection with God that overflows into richer relationships with the people you love.

Sabbath shifts our focus away from ourselves and our challenges and places it squarely on God. In that sacred reorientation, something remarkable happens. We begin to see people as God sees them. Not as interruptions to our productivity or items on our to-do list, but as beloved bearers of His image, worthy of our full attention and care.

Have you been longing for deeper connection with your spouse, your children, your friends? Have you felt the frustration of parallel lives lived under the same roof, ships passing in the night, exchanging logistics but rarely your hearts?

But something different happens at the table during Sabbath.

One Friday evening, out of nowhere, our daughter Tinsley began talking about a friendship struggle she'd been facing. Not the sanitized version she might share with a casual inquiry, but the real emotional landscape—her fear of rejection, her confusion about where she fit. This wasn't information extracted through parental interrogation; it was freely offered, a gift of trust.

Another Sabbath moment I'll never forget, our son Anchor looked around the table after Sabbath and said with surprising clarity, "This is how family is supposed to be." There was something so powerful in that moment. A recognition from a child that this intentional pause wasn't just another activity but a return to the way relationships were designed to function.

These moments don't happen when we're rushing to the next activity or half-listening while multi-tasking. They happen in the sacred spaces we intentionally create.

New Eyes to See

The third transformation: a perspective shift that multiplies creativity and clarity.

Have you noticed how irritable you become when you're rushing? How a slow driver in front of you or a chatty cashier or a spouse who can't find their keys can trigger disproportionate frustration? (I'm a redhead, so I'll be the first to raise my hand!)

That's because hurry diminishes our capacity for love. It constricts our hearts. It reduces complex, valuable humans to obstacles in our path.

When you regularly pause to commune with God and acknowledge what matters most, you start viewing the rest of your week differently.

Things that once seemed urgent begin to lose their power over you. **The email that "can't wait" suddenly can. The house that needs to be "perfectly clean" is actually just fine with a little lived-in messiness.**

I noticed this shift when I stopped apologizing for protecting our Sabbath time. "We're not available Friday evening—that's our family Sabbath." No apology needed for prioritizing what matters most.

But the transformation goes far deeper than just setting better boundaries. **The rhythm of stepping away from endless activity creates space for insights and creativity that eludes us in our productivity mode.**

It's fascinating how our most innovative ideas and clearest thinking often come not when we're striving, but when we're at rest. The solution to a persistent problem, the creative breakthrough, the perspective shift that transforms a relationship challenge—these gifts frequently arrive when we step away from constant doing to simply be with God.

We've experienced this firsthand. Some of our most significant ideas have emerged during or immediately after Sabbath. Michael has found solutions to complex leadership challenges while going for a walk after our Sabbath dinner.

When we step back from our work, we gain a necessary perspective. We can see the forest instead of just the individual trees.

A friend describes this Sabbath-shaped perspective as "putting on God's glasses". This is how we begin to see the world as He sees it, with eternity in view rather than just the urgent demands of the moment. When we return to our regular activities, we carry this enlarged vision with us, making decisions from a place of wisdom rather than reactivity.

We need Sabbath not just for recovery but for revelation. To see what we're otherwise too busy to notice.

Rested and Ready

The fourth transformation might be my favorite: a renewed sense of purpose and the energy to pursue it.

There's something about regularly unplugging from the noise that creates space for clarity about your calling and direction in life. During Sabbath and the days that follow, I often find solutions to problems that had previously seemed insurmountable.

As we explored in the creation story, humans were created at the end of the sixth day, which means their first full day of existence was God's day of rest. Before Adam and Eve did anything, they experienced Sabbath. Before they named a single animal or tended any part of the garden, they rested with God. Their work flowed from their rest, not the other way around.

But let's not forget that God gave them important work to do. He called them to tend the garden, name the animals, and be fruitful. The rest wasn't an escape from purpose but the foundation for it. When work flows from communion with God rather than our own striving, it becomes an expression of worship rather than a burden to bear.

This concept of "working from rest" rather than "resting from work" revolutionizes our approach to productivity.

Have you ever noticed that most fields have seasons of fallowness built into their natural rhythm? Farmers allow fields to lie fallow periodically rather than planting crops every season. This isn't laziness or wasted time. It's essential for the soil to replenish its nutrients.

God designed our minds to need fallow periods too, times when we're not actively producing but are simply being.

We've discovered this same pattern in our own lives. The days following Sabbath have a different quality to them, they're more focused, more purposeful, more aligned. We find ourselves making decisions with greater clarity, setting boundaries with more confidence, and approaching challenges with greater resilience.

The same task approached from depletion feels heavy and draining; approached from renewal, it becomes an expression of purpose and contribution. The work itself hasn't changed, but our relationship to it has been fundamentally altered.

Michael often says, "I get more done in the days after Sabbath than I used to accomplish in seven scattered days." That's not hyperbole; it's the reality of working from a place of rest.

What if the most productive thing you could do this week is to stop, to pause, to reset?

With Sabbath planted squarely in our lives, we find ourselves fighting the right battles, with the right perspective, from the right posture. We're no longer striving from a place of depletion but serving from a place of abundance.

This is where the journey of Sabbath ventures beyond escaping the demands of life; it's about engaging them with renewed vision and strength. The rest and delight of Sabbath aren't the destination but preparation for the meaningful work we're called to do.

From Performance to Presence

Finally, the fifth transformation: from performance to presence.

Sometimes it's hard not to apply my achievement orientation to my relationship with God. Do more, pray more, serve more, read more, learn more. **But Sabbath teaches us that God values our presence more than our performance.**

By simply, wholeheartedly showing up and bringing ourselves to the table, lighting the candles, inviting His presence, breaking the bread, this becomes an act of sacred surrender.

This simple shift from earning to receiving has revolutionized my understanding of grace. When I can receive rest as a gift rather than trying to earn it through productivity, it's a weekly enacted parable of how salvation works. It's how the love of God chases after us.

Have you been trying to earn God's approval? Trying to be "good enough" for His love? **What if the invitation is simply to receive what's already been given? To rest in His presence and allow that communion to transform you from the inside out?**

The Person You're Becoming

Through regular Sabbath rhythms, you will find yourself gradually transforming. Not by trying harder to change, but by consistently placing yourself in the presence of the One who changes you. It's like spending time in the sun: you don't have to work at getting a tan; you simply need to be in the light.

You'll begin to:

> Experience contentment with who you are and what you have

> Strengthen relationships with the people you care about

> Find the ability to focus on what matters most in life

> Renew your mind with a fresh perspective to tackle challenges

> Live from a place of abundance

> Develop natural generosity and curiosity

The transformation goes far beyond a single evening each week.

We no longer feel the need to chase rest through social media, movies or getaways. We still love to do all those things but we don't "need" them because we've found renewal in our weekly rhythm.

Our kids look forward to and relish these slow moments, something extraordinary in our fast-paced world. Our marriage has been strengthened through these meaningful moments of connection. And we've experienced expanded creativity and fresh perspectives that spill into every area of life.

I don't know what transformations Sabbath will bring to your life. Each journey is unique. But I know this: when you create space for God's presence, change is inevitable.

The transformation may not happen overnight. The change may be imperceptible week by week, but over time, the difference becomes unmistakable. Small choices create long-term change.

I'm reminded of how pottery is formed. The clay doesn't transform into something beautiful through brute force but through consistent, gentle pressure applied at the right places over time. **In the same way, the Creator shapes us not through spiritual intensity but through sacred rhythms sustained over time.**

This powerful metaphor reminds us that transformation is God's work in us. We are yielding to the Master Potter's touch as He shapes us into vessels of purpose and beauty. **The Sabbath table becomes His potter's wheel. It's the sacred space where His gentle, skilled hands form us week after week.**

The journey begins with a single step. One evening set apart, one meal shared with intention, one moment of genuine presence with God and those you love.

But here's the reality: the moment you decide to accept this invitation and start Sabbath, don't be surprised if life pushes back against your intention.

And that's when you'll discover what you're truly made of.

WHAT IF THE
RESISTANCE
YOU
FEEL
TOWARD
REST

IS EXACTLY WHY YOU
NEED IT MOST?

CHAPTER ELEVEN

When Reality Fights Back

Something you'll inevitably face on this journey is resistance. The moment you decide to embrace Sabbath, forces both external and internal will push back.

That's because rest is at war—between flesh and spirit.

Jesus warned us that "the thief comes only to steal and kill and destroy; I have come that they may have life, and have it to the full" (John 10:10 NIV). The resistance you'll feel isn't just psychological—it's spiritual warfare against the abundant life God designed you to live. **The enemy of your soul knows that a person connected to their Creator is infinitely more powerful than someone running on empty.**

Understanding this resistance and knowing how to navigate through it, is crucial for establishing a sustainable practice. Let's explore not just the challenges you'll encounter but the breakthroughs that await on the other side of persistence.

I'll never forget one of our first few Sabbaths, everything that could go wrong did.

One of the kids knocked over the grape juice, flooding across our table. The dinner I'd carefully prepared emerged from the oven burnt. Just as we were about to begin the blessing, my phone rang with a work emergency I felt compelled to answer.

By the end of the evening, I was fighting back tears of frustration. "This is supposed to be peaceful," I whispered to Michael as we cleaned up the mess. "Why does it feel like warfare?"

His answer has stayed with me: "Maybe because it is."

Let me be perfectly honest with you: the moment you decide to embrace Sabbath, resistance will come your way.

It's like announcing you're going on a diet right before someone brings chocolate cake to the office. Suddenly, everything around you seems to conspire against your good intention.

Have you ever noticed how the universe seems to sense your commitment to positive change and immediately tests your resolve? It's as if declaring "I'm going to exercise more" triggers an automatic response from your schedule to fill every potential workout slot with urgent meetings. Or deciding "I'm going to be more patient with my children" ensures they'll test every ounce of that patience within hours.

This isn't a coincidence. It's the natural friction that occurs whenever we attempt to change established patterns. And when those patterns involve something as fundamental as how we view and use time (something Sabbath directly challenges), the resistance can be particularly fierce.

This resistance isn't just in your head; it's spiritual. The enemy understands what we often forget: that our greatest power

comes not from pushing harder but from drawing closer to the Source of all strength.

There's a reason Jesus faced opposition when He tried to retreat for prayer, why the Israelites were attacked when they paused to worship, why your most meaningful spiritual commitments face the fiercest opposition. When you decide to create space for God's presence through Sabbath, you're making a declaration in both the visible and invisible realms: "I belong to God, not to the treadmill of productivity." That declaration will be tested, not because you're doing something wrong, but because you're doing something significant.

We've been setting aside this time for over three years now, and I can tell you—the resistance never fully goes away. It just changes form.

The Forms of Resistance

In the beginning, the resistance is obvious and external. The Friday you choose to begin your Sabbath practice will mysteriously become the day everyone wants a piece of your time.

Your phone feels like it's physically vibrating in the drawer you tucked it away in. Even when you check and see there are no notifications, you're convinced you can still hear it ringing. You feel a strange anxiety. What if someone needs me? What if I'm missing something important? What if, what if, what if...

Your mind races with all the "productive" things you could be doing instead. The unfinished work project. The unanswered emails. The laundry that needs folding. The yard that needs attention. Your internal taskmaster, so accustomed to driving you relentlessly, rebels against the command to cease.

Your kids whine about something that makes you agitated. "I'm bored." "Why can't we just watch a movie?" "How much longer do we have to sit here?" Their resistance mirrors your own internal restlessness.

You want to give up. "This isn't working," the voice in your head insists. "It's causing more stress than it's relieving. Let's try again another time when things aren't so hectic."

But here's what we've learned: there is no perfect time. Life will always be hectic. The resistance will always find a way to manifest.

The first Sabbath is the hardest. The second is only slightly easier. By the third, you start to feel the benefits, but the resistance is still strong. It's like your soul is going through withdrawal from the constant stimulation and productivity it's become addicted to.

I remember our fourth Sabbath attempt vividly. The day had gone relatively smoothly. We had prepared in advance, simplifying our expectations. The kids seemed more cooperative. We were starting to find our rhythm.

And then, just as we lit the candles, our lawn care company showed up with mowers and weedwhackers.

The noise was deafening. The peaceful atmosphere we'd carefully cultivated shattered. My initial reaction was frustration verging on anger. Couldn't we have just ONE hour of peace and quiet?

But in that moment, I realized something important: perfect circumstances will never exist. If we waited for optimal conditions to practice Sabbath, we never would. The key wasn't eliminating all external disturbances; it was developing an internal center that couldn't be easily disturbed.

Then there's the social resistance. Friends invite you to Friday evening events. Work schedules expand to fill the space. Family members may not understand why this suddenly matters so much to you.

One Friday, about two months into our Sabbath journey, I received a call from a business colleague. "We need to meet Friday evening," he said. "It's the only time that works."

I felt the pull of people-pleasing, the fear of missing an opportunity, the worry about looking unprofessional. But something deeper had taken root in me, a conviction that this sacred time was worth protecting.

"I'm sorry, but Friday evening doesn't work for me this week," I replied. "How about Monday morning?"

There was a momentary pause while he checked his calendar. I held my breath, waiting for the pushback, the subtle indication that I wasn't being accommodating enough, that my boundaries were inconvenient.

Instead, he simply said, "Monday works. See you then."

That helped me to realize something important: most of the external resistance we anticipate is often nowhere near as strong as the internal resistance we create. The world adjusts to our boundaries far more easily than we expect; it's our own fear of setting them that creates the struggle.

The Internal Battle

As your journey continues, the resistance becomes more subtle. It shifts from external conflicts to internal distractions. You're physically at the table, but your mind is still at work. Your body is present, but your attention is fragmented.

Have you ever been in a conversation while a part of your mind is busy composing an email, planning dinner, or rehashing an earlier conflict? That divided attention is what we bring to so many moments of our lives, including, initially, to Sabbath.

I found myself physically at our Sabbath table but mentally scanning through my to-do list for the weekend. My husband was speaking words of blessing over me, but I was rehearsing an upcoming presentation. Our children were sharing highlights from their week, but I was distracted by the kitchen mess visible from my chair.

Sabbath becomes more than just setting aside time; it becomes setting aside yourself (your striving, your controlling, your endless doing) to simply be in God's presence.

This internal battle reveals something profound: our identity has become so intertwined with productivity that simply being feels foreign, even threatening. Who am I if I'm not doing, achieving, producing? What is my worth apart from what I accomplish?

Sabbath gently but persistently challenges our addiction to doing. Like any addiction recovery, the process isn't comfortable. There are withdrawal symptoms. There's the discomfort of facing what we've been running from or numbing through constant activity. There's the identity crisis that comes when we step away from our primary coping mechanisms.

But as with any healing process, the discomfort is purposeful. It's the necessary path to freedom.

The Illusion of Control

This resistance often manifests in one of its most powerful forms: our desperate grip on the illusion of control.

Michael hit a wall during a particularly intense season of leadership. Multiple high-stakes responsibilities collided with unexpected organizational challenges while leading initiatives that impacted thousands creating an overload of stress. The weight wasn't just heavy; it was suffocating. Leaders know that unique loneliness, when everyone's looking to you for answers while you're secretly wondering if you have anything left to give.

We had the standard leadership survival toolkit: disciplined exercise routines, sleep optimization techniques, carefully scheduled "quick getaways". But they only provided momentary relief. He was managing symptoms while his soul was suffering.

What changed his experience wasn't better time management techniques but deeper communion with God through starting Sabbath. Not trying harder to create margins but surrendering more fully to the One who promises rest for the soul. Not more efficient recovery strategies but a more intimate relationship with our Creator.

For years, he had resisted this kind of surrender. He told himself that resting meant relinquishing control. This is something that feels threatening to someone wired for action and impact. The thought of intentionally pausing felt like weakness, like admitting defeat, like dropping the balls he was so carefully juggling. What would happen if he let go, even briefly? Wouldn't everything fall apart?

Yet something kept inviting him to a different way. Every time he reached the end of his strength, a gentle voice would whisper: "Come to me. Get away with me." It wasn't commanding or demanding. It was an invitation to exchange exhaustion for energy, chaos for clarity.

The hardest part wasn't managing his schedule to create space for Sabbath. The hardest part was surrendering his illusion of control.

Admitting that the world would continue turning without him being available 24/7. That God's purposes would advance even if he paused. That his worth wasn't tied to his endless productivity.

When he finally said, "I can't, but God can," something shifted. Not in his circumstances, but in his heart. The yoke that had been crushing him was replaced with one he could actually bear—because he wasn't bearing it alone.

This struggle with control isn't unique to us. It's one of the most common forms of resistance we all face. Our society celebrates those who maintain control, who never show weakness, who power through every obstacle. Sabbath directly confronts this illusion by inviting us to acknowledge our limitations and depend on God's limitless strength.

Seasons of Struggle

About a year into our journey, we hit a challenging season. Work demands were intense, our kids' schedules were packed, and I found myself thinking, "We just need to get through this busy period, then we can get back to consistent Sabbath time."

I started viewing Sabbath as something we did when life allowed, rather than a non-negotiable that shaped our life's rhythm. It became the thing we'd "get back to" when circumstances improved.

That's when Michael said something that stopped me in my tracks: "What if Sabbath isn't the thing we do when life calms down, but the very thing that would help us navigate this chaos?"

He was right. **We were falling into the same trap we had been in before—seeing rest as a reward for completion rather than the foundation for creation. We were back to earning what had been freely given.**

Have you noticed how we tend to approach rest in our culture? It's the carrot at the end of the stick, always just out of reach. "I'll rest when this project is finished." "I'll take time off after this busy season." "I'll focus on my family once I get this promotion." But the project leads to another project, the busy season extends indefinitely, and the promotion brings more responsibility rather than more margin.

That week, we recommitted to our rhythm. It wasn't elaborate. We lit a candle, and turned off our phones. But that simple act of pressing pause made all the difference.

I remember the weight that lifted from my shoulders that evening, not because our circumstances had changed, but because our perspective had. We weren't waiting for life to provide the perfect conditions for peace; we were creating a space for peace in the midst of imperfect conditions.

Practical Ways to Press Through

So how do we push through this resistance?

Three things have helped us persevere when everything in us wanted to abandon this journey:

1. **Start simple.** In seasons of intense resistance, don't abandon the practice. Simplify it. A single candle, a simple blessing, a few minutes of silence. These small acts of obedience create space for God to work even when the full practice feels impossible.

2. **Acknowledge the resistance out loud.** Name it without shame: "I'm noticing I feel anxious about turning off my phone" or "I feel resistance to slowing down right now." Simply naming what's happening diminishes its power and prevents it from operating in the shadows

3. **Remember why this matters.** When resistance is strongest, return to your deepest motivation. For us, it was witnessing the transformation in our children, the anchoring of our marriage, the recovery of wonder in ordinary moments. Your "why" will carry you through when willpower alone cannot.

The Breakthrough Beyond

The resistance you feel is real. But so is the rest, delight, and activation waiting on the other side. The breakthrough rarely happens dramatically. It's usually not a single moment where everything suddenly clicks. Instead, it's a gradual transition, like dawn slowly dispelling darkness.

In our experience, it happened over months. We noticed small shifts: the kids asking when Sabbath would begin rather than fussing about it. The preparation becomes more joyful and less stressful. The conversations deepened. The resistance, while still present, loses its power to derail us.

After pushing through those initial weeks of newness and resistance, Sabbath has become the rhythm our family's hearts beat to. We still face challenges. We still experience resistance. But now there's something deeper pulling us back to the table each week. It's the peace we experience there, but the purpose it unlocks in every other area of our lives.

This is the beautiful completion of the Sabbath Soul Cycle we discovered earlier: we press pause from the chaos, find rest in God's presence, discover delight in authentic connection, and activate purpose that transforms how we engage the world. Each week, these sacred rhythm deepens, moving us from reactive living to intentional engagement.

What began as a spiritual discipline has become essential. What felt like a struggle has become a delight. What seemed like weakness is actually wisdom.

This is the full circle of Sabbath's design: what starts as a retreat from the world becomes our launchpad into it. The four rhythms don't just restore us, they propel us forward with renewed clarity, creativity, compassion, and conviction that we could never manufacture in our own strength.

The resistance never fully disappears, but it no longer defines the experience. Like a musician who has practiced long enough that the scales and technical exercises become second nature, allowing the true artistry to emerge, we find that the mechanical aspects of Sabbath fade into the background while its true purpose comes to the foreground.

The Gift is the Reward

Every meaningful change encounters resistance. Every worthwhile journey includes obstacles. Every transformation requires pushing through initial discomfort.

Sabbath is no exception.

But on the other side of that resistance lies a gift worth fighting for. A rhythm that can transform not just your week, but your entire approach to life, work, and relationships. The very intensity of the resistance you feel is often proportional to the significance of what awaits you beyond it.

Friends of ours shared, "Sabbath didn't just press pause on our chaos; it completely rewired our family's operating system," shared a friend and sleep-deprived dad with a newborn. "Turns out, choosing to stop isn't weakness; it's where your real strength has been hiding all along!"

Remember this: the resistance you'll face isn't an indicator that you're doing something wrong—it's evidence that you're disrupting patterns that need to be broken, challenging assumptions that need to be questioned, and creating space for a divine encounter that the world around you desperately wants to crowd out.

The invitation to Sabbath isn't just about what you'll stop doing—it's about Who you'll start encountering in the space created by your pause. The resistance you will feel is real. But so is what is waiting on the other side.

EXTRAORDINARY THINGS HAPPEN

WHEN YOU DARE TO PAUSE

"

CHAPTER TWELVE

Your Sacred Invitation

I nearly missed it.

Sitting in my inbox was the invitation to Israel that would change everything. Where the Lord would reveal His sacred invitation to rest.

I wonder if you're at a similar threshold now. This book in your hands is no coincidence. Like that email I almost overlooked, these pages contain an invitation that could transform everything. I urge you not to dismiss it, not to file it away for "someday when life calms down."

The gift of Sabbath is an invitation to experience life as it was meant to be lived, not someday, but starting this week.

Vision for Redemptive Renewal

Here's something that's been stirring in my heart as we consider the transformative power of Sabbath: I've noticed that when it comes to the Ten Commandments, most of us naturally follow nine of them. We know it's wrong to murder, and we instinctively know that honoring our parents and treating God's name with reverence matters deeply. Yet somehow, the fourth commandment to remember the Sabbath and keep it holy has quietly slipped from our collective consciousness.

I don't think this happened intentionally. Life just got busier, weekends filled up, and somewhere along the way, this ancient rhythm began to feel optional rather than essential.

But what if there's a connection between setting aside this divine rhythm and many of the struggles we're facing today?

When I look around at the epidemic of mental health challenges, the fragility of so many marriages, the disconnect between parents and children, I can't help but wonder: could it be that in our well-meaning busyness, we've unknowingly removed a cornerstone that was designed to support human flourishing?

We imagine a movement where Sabbath becomes a quiet revolution against the forces of exhaustion, distraction, and spiritual depletion that characterize our age.

We picture communities where families regularly disconnect from the digital chaos to reconnect with what matters most. Where children grow up knowing there's more to life than achievement and acquisition. Where relationships deepen through unhurried presence. Where souls find regular renewal through communion with their Creator.

The ripple effects would transform everything:

Our **mental health** would flourish as people discover the healing and restoration that comes through regular rhythms of rest and meaningful connection. The simple practice of stepping away from constant stimulation and pressure creates space for our minds to recover and reset.

Our **marriages** would be fortified through intentional togetherness beyond logistics and problem-solving. The weekly practice of looking into each other's eyes, speaking words of blessing, and unhurried presence creates a sacred bond that withstands the inevitable storms of life. Couples would find themselves reconnecting at a soul level, remembering why they chose each other.

Our **family systems** would strengthen as parents and children create memories and traditions around the Sabbath table. These moments become anchors of stability in an increasingly fragmented culture, forming the stories that shape family identity for generations.

Our **churches** would experience revitalization as members move from religious obligation to genuine communion with God. Worship becomes more authentic when flowing from hearts renewed through regular Sabbath practice. Service becomes more effective when emerging from rest than pressure.

Our **workplaces** would witness a revolution in productivity and creativity as people bring renewed perspective and energy to their vocations. The paradox of Sabbath is that by working less, we often accomplish more, not by increasing hours but by enhancing focus, clarity, and purpose.

Our **witness** would intensify as our light becomes visible to a world desperate for hope in the darkness. When people ask, "Why do you live differently?" we have the opportunity to share about the God who designed us for more than endless productivity.

This isn't daydreaming.

Cultural transformation begins with individual transformation: not through grand gestures, but through consistent choices that gradually reshape the landscape of our collective experience.

One table at a time. One family at a time. One community at a time.

Sharing the Light

The beauty of Sabbath is that it transcends socioeconomic status and cultural background. Around the world, every Friday evening, millions of lights begin to flicker on (one by one, home by home), creating a constellation of sacred moments that spans continents and connects hearts.

Imagine that at the same moment you gather at the table...

A family in a rural Guatemalan village is gathering around a wooden table adorned with handwoven runners passed down through generations, using simple clay cups that connect them to their ancestors' practices.

College students across university towns gather in apartments, transforming ordinary tables into sacred spaces with shared meals. They've created a ritual of disconnection with phones away in a large mixing bowl as they rediscover the art of unhurried conversation over breaking bread together.

In a high-rise overlooking the city skyline, a professional has stepped away from urgent business demands to gather her family around an elegantly set table with fine china that belonged to her grandmother.

A single parent has established a weekly technology-free zone in their home, where despite the challenges of solo parenting, they've made Friday evenings non-negotiable. With a thoughtfully arranged tablecloth that only comes out for Sabbath, they're teaching their children that some moments are worth protecting at all costs.

Refugees who fled their homeland create sacred space in temporary housing that speaks of resilience, hope, and continuity.

In a retirement community, elderly residents have gathered in a common room, where decades of wisdom are shared across a table set with collected treasures, each item telling a story of faith preserved through changing times.

Each flame, each table, each gathering speaks a similar truth: this time is set apart. The physical elements aren't about expense or status; they're visual cues that this meal transcends the ordinary. The setting is a tangible reminder that this time is different, regardless of your resources or circumstances.

And though separated by distance, culture, and circumstance, all who practice this rhythm are united in a countercultural pause against the chaos of hustle culture.

A Table Set for Every Nation

There's something profound happening when we consider Isaiah's prophetic words: "From one Sabbath to another, all mankind will come and bow down before me, says the LORD" (Isaiah 66:23 NIV). This isn't just a distant promise, it's being fulfilled right now, one table at a time, as believers from every nation gather to break bread and commune with their Creator.

What if part of honoring this global fellowship means celebrating the rich culinary traditions that different cultures bring to the Sabbath table?

Picture the beautiful mosaic of flavors and aromas rising as offerings to God around the world each Friday evening.

In Mexico, families gather around tables laden with fresh tortillas, slow-cooked carnitas, and vibrant salsas: their Sabbath meal a fiesta of gratitude for God's provision.

Korean believers might share bulgogi and kimchi, the fermented vegetables representing patience and the transformation that comes through time, much like our own spiritual growth through consistent Sabbath practice.

Italian families pass plates of handmade pasta and rich marinara, each recipe carrying stories passed down through generations, now sanctified through sacred intention.

Ethiopian communities break injera bread together, using their hands to share from communal plates, a beautiful picture of the unity we have in Christ.

Southern American tables might feature slow-cooked collard greens, cornbread, and fried chicken: comfort foods that speak of hospitality and the Father's welcoming heart.

Indian families create aromatic curries, fragrant rice, and warm naan, each spice a reminder of the complexity and richness of God's creation.

This diversity isn't just cultural appreciation; it's prophetic participation. When we intentionally incorporate dishes from different cultures into our Sabbath meals, we're living into the reality that God's table is set for every tribe, tongue, and nation.

Consider hosting a "Nations Sabbath" where you prepare a meal from a different culture, pray for that nation, and learn about how believers there experience God's presence. Let your children help research the country, prepare the food, and discover how their brothers and sisters in Christ gather around tables thousands of miles away.

In doing so, you're not just expanding your palate; you're expanding your heart to embrace the global family of faith that will one day feast together at the marriage supper of the Lamb.

Your Personal Invitation

As you consider this invitation, you might be thinking, "This sounds wonderful, but will it really work for someone like me?" Wherever you find yourself today, know that Sabbath has room for your heart...

For the Anxious Heart

Dear one with the burdened mind and weary soul,

I see you—behind the carefully composed smile, beneath the "I'm fine" you offer when asked how you're doing. Those **F**eelings **I**nside, **N**ot **E**xpressed that build up day after day. I see the overwhelming worry, the thoughts that spin like never-ending wheels. The way anxiety wakes you at night and follows you through your days. The exhaustion of living on high alert, always scanning for the next threat, the next problem, the next disappointment.

You've tried so many remedies, haven't you? The breathing techniques that work for a moment but can't calm the deeper storm. The self-help books that don't reach the root of your fear. The coping mechanisms that take the edge off but leave you feeling empty. The distractions that provide temporary relief but offer no lasting peace.

I created Sabbath as a sanctuary for you. A weekly reminder that you don't have to carry the weight of the world. For one sacred day, let Me carry your burdens. Let Me quiet your racing thoughts. Let Me remind you who you are and whose you are.

At My table, you'll find the peace that eludes you everywhere else. Not because your circumstances have changed, but because you've encountered the Prince of Peace. Your soul was designed for rhythms of rest, not living on high alert.

Come away with Me. Your anxious heart will find its home in My perfect love.

For the Spiritual Seeker

Beloved searcher,

I see your hunger for something deeper, something real. The way you've tried to fill that God-shaped void with religious activities, spiritual practices, or intellectual pursuits. The disappointment when each new approach falls short of the connection you crave.

You've explored so many paths, haven't you? The meditation apps that promised centering but left you feeling more scattered. The worship experiences that stirred emotion but faded by Monday morning. The studies that expanded your mind but didn't necessarily open your heart. The service projects that helped others but somehow left you feeling emptier.

I designed Sabbath as a pathway to My presence. Not another ritual to perfect, but a relationship to enjoy. **At My table,** the veil between heaven and earth grows thin. The sacred and ordinary merge. The God you've been seeking comes to meet you right where you are.

This is what you've been looking for all along. Not more information about Me, but actual communion with Me. Not distant worship, but intimate fellowship.

Come away with Me. Your seeking soul will find its rest in My presence.

For the Driven Professional

My dedicated child,

I see your tireless work, your commitment to excellence, your desire to make a difference in your field. I also see the toll it's taking—the way achievement has become your identity, productivity your worth, success your security.

You've accomplished so much, haven't you? The career milestones, the professional recognition, the financial rewards. You've pushed through exhaustion, sacrificed personal time, extended yourself beyond reasonable limits. You've built something impressive, but at what cost?

I created Sabbath as a declaration of your true value. A weekly reminder that you are infinitely precious to Me, completely apart from what you accomplish. **At My table,** you'll discover what it means to simply be rather than always do. To receive rather than achieve. To know that you are loved not for what you can do but for who you are.

This pressing pause will not diminish your effectiveness but multiply it. The time that seems "lost" to rest is actually investing in a more focused, creative, and purposeful use of all your other hours.

Come away with Me. Your seeking soul will find its rest in My presence.

For the Loving Parent

My faithful steward,

I see your deep love for your children, your desire to give them everything they need, your worry that you're not doing enough. I see the exhaustion behind your smile, the questioning behind your confidence, the weight of responsibility you carry.

You've given so much, haven't you? The sleepless nights, the emotional energy, the never-ending adjusting to their changing needs. The research into the best approaches, the consistent attempts to do better than was done for you. The juggling of their needs with everything else demanding your attention.

I designed Sabbath as a gift for your family. A weekly inheritance more valuable than any material provision. **At My table,** you'll model for your children what matters most. You'll create spaces for authentic connection. You'll build memories and traditions that will shape their understanding of faith long after they leave your home.

This isn't another parenting technique to master; it's an invitation to bring your family into the rhythm of grace I designed from the beginning of time. Your children don't need a perfect parent, they need one who knows how to receive and give love from an overflow.

Come away with Me. Your parent's heart will find its confidence in My Father's love.

From Our Table to Yours

As we sit here writing these final words, we're filled with a sense of hope for you. **Hope that you'll discover what we've found: that there is extraordinary peace in ordinary moments.** That in a culture of constant noise, there is a peace that comes from a mind steadfast on God, just as Isaiah wrote: "You will keep in perfect peace those whose minds are steadfast, because they trust in you" (Isaiah 26:3 NIV). That in the midst of life's inevitable storms, there is an anchor that holds us safe.

Our Sabbath journey has brought the beautiful sacred rhythms of pressing pause, finding rest, discovering delight, and activating purpose into our hearts, filling them with peace and wholeness that has overflowed into every aspect of our lives. We've learned that true rest isn't an escape from reality but preparation for it. That genuine delight isn't a fleeting emotion but a doorway to deeper purpose. That the most meaningful work flows from a place of connection rather than striving.

The table where we began this practice has become for us a space where heaven and earth seem to touch, where the eternal breaks into the temporal, where the sacred transforms the ordinary. It's the still point in our turning world, the stable center that holds everything else in proper perspective.

Perhaps your table will become this for you too. Not overnight, not without effort, not without moments of doubt and resistance. But gradually, meaningfully, transformatively.

Remember that your journey will be uniquely yours. Your practice will reflect your family's personality, your specific circumstances, your particular relationship with God. The beauty of Sabbath is found not in perfect replication but in authentic expression: capturing the heart of divine rest in ways that resonate with your specific situation.

Sabbath is the gift God gave us we didn't even know we needed—and it's one that's been waiting for you since the beginning of time.

As you close this book, we challenge you to open your calendar and mark your first Sabbath. This coming Friday would be a great time (or choose a time that works for your rhythm of life).

The table is set. The invitation is extended. And Jesus awaits at the table.

To your Sabbath story,
Michael & Selah

The Gift You Carry Everywhere

Once this sacred rhythm takes root in your heart, it travels with you everywhere. We discovered this truth 4,000 miles from home on an island in the Pacific Ocean.

Michael was days away from racing the Ironman World Championship in Kona, Hawaii (his childhood dream, thirteen years in the making). The week had been a whirlwind. Gear check-in. Tourist activities. Wrangling kids while managing vacation excitement and race day nerves.

Friday evening came, as it always does.

Extended family and friends who had journeyed with us gathered on the patio. As the sun set in brilliant yellow and orange hues, we lit the candles.

The spirit of Sabbath rose up in our hearts. Words of affirmation brought tears to our eyes as we pressed pause to recognize God's presence. This treasured time meant even more than the celebration at the finish line.

You have the ability to create holy ground wherever you are. To transform any table into an altar. To press pause and find divine presence in any moment.

Whether you're celebrating a mountaintop moment or navigating an unexpected valley, whether you're gathered around your grandmother's table or balancing paper plates on your lap, **Sabbath creates space for God to meet you exactly where you are.**

The invitation always stands for you to press pause and discover God waiting for you at the table.

Start Sabbath

Millions are choosing a different way.

They're trading constant commotion for sacred pause. A revolution is spreading, one table at a time, and it's absolutely beautiful.

Start Sabbath is creating space for God's presence to transform:

> Exhausted minds into wellsprings of clarity

> Disconnected hearts into vessels of compassion

> Fragmented attention into focused presence

> Spiritual dryness into abundant wonder

What's amazing is that people will notice the peace we carry. They'll wonder about our boundaries and clarity. But they'll be drawn to the way we approach life from abundance rather than depletion. It's countercultural and full of contagious joy.

While you've been reading this, families around the world have been gathering at their Sabbath table. Others are planning their first time at the table this week. **The movement is happening, and it's infinitely richer with you as part of it.**

Don't go another week running ragged. Join thousands taking the Press Pause Challenge right now. Commit to just one Sabbath meal this week. Turn off your phone. Speak a blessing. **It's that simple and life-changing.**

Take the Press Pause Challenge today at www.startsabbath.com

Sabbath Starter Guide

A simple outline to begin your journey

This guide provides the essential steps to create your first Sabbath experience. Remember, there's no "perfect" way to practice Sabbath. Authenticity matters more than execution. Start here and let your unique rhythm develop over time.

STEP 1
Prepare Your Heart & Space

> Turn off phones and silence devices
> Take a deep breath and shift from "doing" to "being"
> Set the table with intention
  (candles, special dishes, or simply what you have)
> Prepare or order your meal

STEP 2
Welcome God's Presence

> Gather everyone and say "Shabbat Shalom" (Sabbath Peace)

> Share a brief devotional—read a Bible verse or share what God did in your week

> Light candles and say "We welcome God's presence as we begin our Sabbath"

> Invite each person to share one thing they're grateful for

Step 3
Speak Blessing Over Each Other

> Look each person in the eyes

> Tell them something specific you appreciate about them this week

> Say together: "May God's blessing be upon each person here."

Step 4
Share Cup & Bread

> Bless the cup: "Thank you for this cup of the new covenant"

> Bless the bread: "We do this, Jesus, in remembrance of you"

> Enjoy your meal together without rushing

Step 5
Linger & Connect

> Stay at the table after eating

> Ask meaningful questions or share stories

> Let conversation flow naturally—no agenda needed

For more explanation, see Chapter 8: Simple Steps to Start

Sample Blessings

Words to speak life and identity over those you love

The practice of blessing others is both ancient and revolutionary—it transforms not just the receiver but also the giver. As you develop the habit of looking for the divine image in others, your own vision enlarges.

Biblical Blessings

For Boys: (Based on Genesis 48:20 - Jacob's blessing over Ephraim and Manasseh): "May God make you like Ephraim and Manasseh. May the God before whom my fathers Abraham and Isaac walked faithfully, the God who has been my shepherd all my life to this day, bless you. May you carry forward the faith of generations and become a blessing to many."

For Girls: (Based on the Matriarchs): "May God make you like Sarah, Rebecca, Rachel, and Leah. May you walk in wisdom and strength, in faithfulness and courage. May you know your identity as a daughter of the King and become a woman who builds her household in the fear of the Lord."

General Templates

"[Name], I see [specific quality] in you. This week when you [specific action], it showed me what a [affirming adjective] person you are. May God [specific blessing for their future]."

"[Name], you reflect God's [attribute] when you [example]. I'm grateful for how you [specific contribution]. May you always know how deeply you are [loved/valued/treasured]."

Sample Blessings Continued

For Children

"[Name], I see in you a beautiful gift of [specific quality]. This week, I noticed when you [specific action]. You are deeply loved by God and by us. May you always know your worth and your purpose."

"May you grow in wisdom and confidence, knowing you are never alone. May you recognize your unique gifts and find joy in using them. May you know how deeply you are loved, not for what you do but for who you are."

For Spouse/Partner

"[Name], I am grateful for your [specific quality]. This week when you [specific action], it showed me again the person of integrity and love that you are. Thank you for journeying with me. May you feel God's pleasure in who you are."

"I see your strength when you face challenges and your tenderness when you respond to pain. I honor the way you [specific quality or action]. May you know how deeply valued you are, how specifically needed, how particularly loved."

For Friends/Guests

"[Name], you bring such [specific quality] to our lives. I've been blessed by your [specific impact]. May you know how valued you are and experience God's peace in every area of your life."

Sample Blessings Continued

For Self-Blessing (When Practicing Alone)

"I am God's beloved child, created in His image and cherished by Him. Today I recognize the gift of [quality] that God has placed within me. This week when I [action], I reflected something of God's character. I receive His grace for my weaknesses and His delight in my growth."

For Specific Seasons

In Transition: "May God go before you into this new season. May you find unexpected blessings in unfamiliar places. May you carry forward all that has been good while remaining open to fresh wisdom."

In Grief: "May you feel God's tender presence in your sorrow. May you find comfort in precious memories and hope in eternal promises. May you be gentle with yourself as you navigate this valley."

In Celebration: "May your joy be multiplied as you share it. May this season of blessing remind you of God's faithful love. May you store up these moments as treasures to sustain you."

In Uncertainty: "May you find solid ground in God's unchanging character when everything else seems shifting. May wisdom guide your decisions and peace guard your heart."

Conversation Starters

Questions to deepen connection around your table

Meaningful conversation is the heart of Sabbath connection. These starters are organized by theme to help you move from surface exchanges to soul-level sharing.

Gratitude & Joy

> What made you smile this week?

> What's something small you enjoyed today?

> When have you felt most grateful recently?

Identity & Purpose

> What activity makes you lose track of time?

> When do you feel most like your authentic self?

> What would you like to be known for?

Growth & Learning

> What's something new you learned recently?

> What mistake taught you something valuable?

> How are you different now than a year ago?

Wonder & Creativity

> What's something beautiful you noticed recently?

> When have you experienced awe or wonder?

> What creative expression helps you connect with God?

Relationships & Community

> Who made a positive difference in your day?

> How has someone's love helped you understand God's love better?

> Who would you like to thank right now and why?

Rest & Renewal

> What helps you relax when you're stressed?

> What makes it difficult for you to truly rest?

> Where is your "quiet place" with Jesus?

Scripture-Based Conversations

> "The Lord is my shepherd; I shall not want." (Psalm 23:1) What "green pastures" has God provided in your life?

> "Come with me by yourselves to a quiet place and get some rest." (Mark 6:31) Where or when do you experience this invitation?

> "I have come that they may have life, and have it to the full." (John 10:10) What does a "full life" look like to you?

Remember When...

> What's a favorite Sabbath memory we've shared?

> What blessing from a previous Sabbath has stayed with you?

> How has our time together changed how you experience the rest of the week?

Common Questions

Thoughtful responses to help you navigate your journey

As you begin your Sabbath journey, questions will naturally arise. Here are thoughtful responses to common concerns that might emerge as you develop your own practice.

Q: "We have sports/activities on Friday nights."

A: This is reality for many families. Consider adopting a flexible approach—perhaps your Sabbath happens on Saturday morning or Sunday evening. The key is consistency and intentionality, not the specific day or time.

Q: "I don't know the prayers or traditions."

A: Start with just three elements: lighting a candle, saying what you're grateful for, and blessing each other. From that simple beginning, you can gradually develop your own meaningful experience that honors the spirit of Sabbath while reflecting your unique faith background and family culture.

Q: "I'm not sure my family will get on board."

A: Start small. Introduce elements gradually. Focus on the aspects most likely to resonate with your family members. For some, it might be the special meal. For others, the blessing.

Q: "How do I involve teenagers who might resist?"

A: Give them ownership by inviting their input on aspects of Sabbath that matter to them. Perhaps they choose the music, help plan the meal, or select an evening activity. Many teens respond to authentic explanation—share why this matters to you personally instead of imposing it as a rule. Also, consider giving them specific meaningful roles that tap into their strengths.

Q: Is this just a Jewish practice?

A: While Sabbath has deep roots in Jewish tradition, it predates Judaism itself. God established the seventh-day rhythm at creation before any formal religious structure existed. Jesus himself regularly participated in Sabbath while clarifying its true purpose of restoration. Christians throughout history have observed various forms of Sabbath as a spiritual discipline central to faith formation.

Q: Are we supposed to observe Sabbath on Saturday or Sunday?

A: The specific day matters less than the regular rhythm. Traditionally, the Jewish Sabbath runs from Friday sunset to Saturday sunset, while many Christians observe Sunday as the Lord's Day. What's most important is establishing a consistent time set apart for God. Choose what works best for your family's schedule and cultural context.

Q: If Jesus fulfilled the law, do Christians still need to observe Sabbath?

A: While Christians aren't bound by Old Testament regulations, we're still invited into the wisdom of God's created rhythms. Jesus didn't abolish Sabbath but restored its purpose as a life-giving practice instead of a restrictive obligation. Paul writes in Colossians 2:16, "Therefore do not let anyone judge you by what you eat or drink, or with regard to a religious festival, a New Moon celebration or a Sabbath day." This wasn't dismissing Sabbath as irrelevant, but rather freeing believers from legalistic judgment about how or when they observe it.

Q: How do I know if our Sabbath practice is "working"?

A: Look for subtle changes over time instead of dramatic immediate results:

> Do family members begin to anticipate and prepare for Sabbath?

> Are conversations becoming deeper or more meaningful?

> Do you notice more patience or peace carrying over into the rest of the week?

> Is there a sense of genuine connection with God during this time?

These gradual transformations signal that Sabbath is taking root in your family's rhythm.

Q: What if Sabbath consistently feels like more stress than peace?

A: Simplify your approach. Strip back to the very basics—perhaps just a meal with candles and a simple blessing. Evaluate what elements are creating pressure and adjust or temporarily remove them. Sometimes the stress comes from expectations, not the practice itself. Ask: "What's the minimum needed for this to feel set apart?" and start there.

Q: How do we recover when Sabbath gets derailed?

A: Acknowledge the disruption without shame, then gently reset. If an argument erupts or chaos ensues, take a collective breath and say something like, "Let's begin again." Sometimes the most powerful moments happen when we model how to return to sacred space after disruption. This teaches children (and reminds us) that peace isn't about perfect circumstances but about intentional return.

Q: What if I feel more distant from God during this time?

A: Spiritual dryness visits everyone periodically. During these seasons, lean on the structure and community aspects of Sabbath while being honest about your experience. Sometimes continuing the outward practice creates space for the inward connection to gradually return. Consider sharing your experience with a trusted friend or spiritual director who can offer perspective.

Q: How do I avoid turning Sabbath into another legalistic practice?

A: Keep the focus on relationship over performance. Notice when you're evaluating "success" based on execution instead of connection. Regularly ask, "Is this creating space for God's presence and meaningful relationship?" not "Are we doing this correctly?" Welcome adaptations, maintain flexibility, and let delight take precedence over duty.

Q: What if I miss several weeks in a row?

A: Extend to yourself the grace you would offer anyone else. The invitation to return remains open without penalty or shame. Sometimes a longer gap requires a simple "reset" conversation: "I've missed our Sabbath time and want to begin again." Treat each return as a welcome homecoming, not a makeup test.

Q: How do we handle it when family members are reluctant or resistant?

A: Sabbath has a naturally life-giving effect that draws people in. Focus on the elements that bring joy instead of enforcing compliance. Be willing to start small—while keeping the invitation open.

Thank Yous

As we reflect on this Sabbath journey, we're overwhelmed with gratitude for the divine orchestration that brought this life-changing practice into our lives.

A very special thank you to Mom and Dad Davis, Rabbi Curt and Christie Landry, the Franke family, Paul and Megann Marcellino, Samuel and Lauren Bentley. Each of you represents a divine breadcrumb strategically placed in our path. God was chasing after our hearts, and you helped Him get our attention.

Bishop Robert Stearns and the Eagles Wings team—your invitation to Israel became the cornerstone moment transforming not just our family but launching the Start Sabbath movement.

The generosity of David Nekrutman, the Executive Director of The Isaiah Projects and Founder of Biblical Excavations as well as Reverend Emilie & Craig Wierda and The Ingathering helped to bring this project to life. Their "yes" has created ripples of transformation, a powerful reminder that we never know what a single "yes" will do.

To the Etsebeth family, Henson family, Armstrong family, Pierce family, Nancy Hirsch, and Micah and Andrea Davis, thank you for journeying alongside us. Your community has made Sabbath so much richer.

Our children—Nya, Anchor, Tinsley, and Asher—who embrace this practice with childlike faith. Your enthusiasm for Sabbath reminds us of its power.

And to you, our new friend, thank you for your willingness to consider a countercultural rhythm that might transform your life as it has transformed ours. Our hope is that your Sabbath table will become the place where someone else discovers the gift they didn't know they needed—where the divine breadcrumbs you leave help another find their way home to sacred rest.

That's how God works, taking our small acts of faithful presence and weaving them into His beautiful story of redemption and renewal, one table at a time.

With grateful hearts,

Michael & Selah

About the Authors

Michael and Selah Hirsch are the founders of Start Sabbath, helping leaders, achievers, and families around the world discover the rhythms of sacred rest.

Married nearly 20 years, they perfected the art of productive living. Michael is a world champion Ironman triathlete with decades of experience leading nonprofit organizations. Selah runs a thriving brand agency while overseeing the schedules of their four children. Their life was color-coded calendars, optimized routines, and maximum output on minimal sleep.

When they discovered the gift of Sabbath, it became their anchor during one of the most challenging seasons of their life and leadership. Creating space for God's presence became a lifeline in the storm.

They continue learning, adjusting, and discovering new depths in their Sabbath practice with their four children—Nya, Anchor, Tinsley, and Asher—where their dining table has become holy ground and Friday evenings are the most anticipated part of their week.

Still driven. Still growing. Still building.
Just from a completely different source.

From Our Table to Yours

We get the sweetest photos from friends gathering at their Sabbath tables and it fills our hearts every time!

We'd love to see your sacred space and celebrate with you. Plus, we often share these beautiful glimpses to inspire others on their own Sabbath journey.

Text us a photo at 〜〰↗ **405-397-9576**

Get in Touch!
✉ **michael@startsabbath.com selah@startsabbath.com**

📷 📘 **@startsabbath**

🖥 **www.startsabbath.com**

www.ingramcontent.com/pod-product-compliance
Lightning Source LLC
Chambersburg PA
CBHW010939120626
46554CB00008B/2528